Rose Reisman Brings Home Spa Desserts

Low-Calorie Recipes from Top Resorts Made Easy

by Rose Reisman

Andrews and McMeel

A Universal Press Syndicate Company

Kansas City • New York

Library of Congress Cataloging-in-Publication Data

Reisman, Rose.
    Rose Reisman brings home spa desserts : low-calorie recipes from top resorts made
      easy.
      p.   cm.
    Includes index.
    ISBN 0-8362-2105-2 : $10.95
    1. Low-calorie diet—Recipes. 2. Desserts. I. Title.
RM222.2.R453   1991
641.8'6—dc20   91-7269
                                                            CIP

Book design by Rick Cusick

Attention: Schools and Businesses
Andrews and McMeel books are available at quantity discounts with bulk purchase for educational, business, or sales promotional use. For information, please write to: Special Sales Department, Andrews and McMeel, 4900 Main Street, Kansas City, Missouri 64112.

To diet dessert doubters everywhere (not long ago, I, too, was one of you); to the health conscious individuals concerned with the quality of their lives; and to those who have tried my past dessert decadence . . . here's the antidote!

As ever . . . to my wonderful husband, Sam, and my three perfect children, Natalie, David, and Laura.

Contents

Acknowledgments xi

Introduction xii

Some Healthy Advice 1

Helpful Hints 10

FOUR SEASONS RESORT AND CLUB (Texas) 13
　　Lemon Meringue Pie / Coffee Chiffon Cake
　　Hot Spiced Apples over Honey Vanilla Ice Cream
　　Poached Pears with Blueberry Yogurt Sauce
　　Honey Glazed Pineapple with Strawberries

CANYON RANCH (Arizona and Massachusetts) 19
　　Blueberry Cheesecake
　　"Chokolate" Carob Cake with Pastry Cream / Lemon Frost
　　Carrot Buttermilk Cake / Pumpkin Cheesecake
　　Key Lime Dessert / Zucchini Pineapple Bread
　　Fresh Fruit Sorbet / Raisin Rice Pudding
　　Strawberries Romanoff / Fruit Blintzes / Crêpes

GOLDEN DOOR (California) 33
　　Raspberry Cheesecake / Chocolate Seashells
　　Pear Apple Croustade / Blueberry Apple Sorbet
　　Strawberry Orange Sorbet / Orange Grand Marnier Sorbet

PALM-AIRE (Florida) 39
　　Angel Food Strawberry Shortcake / Baked Alaska
　　Chocolate Angel Food Cake / Five Minute Chocolate Mousse
　　Mixed Fruit Mousse

SHERATON BONAVENTURE RESORT AND SPA (Florida) 45
　　Crêpes Suzette / Blueberry Crêpes
　　Baked Cinnamon Fruit Coupe

THE POINTE (Arizona)   49
    Tarte Tartin / Poached Pears in Chocolate Sauce
    Strawberry Cheese Tart / Oatmeal Maple Raisin Cookies
    Individual Sweet Apple Cakes

SONOMA MISSION INN (California)   55
    Cocoa Kisses / Vanilla Almond Snaps
    Frozen Lemon Chiffon with Berry Sauce
    Chilled Mocha Mousse / Crisp Nut Cookies
    Berry Strudel with Papaya Sauce / Lady Fingers
    Light and Lovely Cheesecake / Raspberry Cream Sorbet

SAFETY HARBOR (Florida)   65
    Individual Miniature Cheesecakes / Applesauce Spice Cake
    Banana Walnut Bread / Fresh Fruit Tart / Bananas Flambé

TURNBERRY ISLE YACHT AND COUNTRY CLUB (Florida)   71
    Peanut Butter Cookies / Raisin Honey Cookies
    Chewy Cottage Cheese Cookies

LA COSTA HOTEL AND SPA (California)   75
    Cinnamon Fig Cake / Peach Melba
    La Costa Cheesecake with Strawberry Sauce

THE GREENHOUSE (Arizona)   79
    Fluffy Apricot Soufflé with Raspberry Sauce
    Crunchy Apple Cobbler / Homemade Crunchy Granola
    Fruit Kabobs with Raspberry Sauce
    Strawberry Orange Buttermilk Sorbet

THE SPA AT TOPNOTCH (Vermont)   85
    Fruit Terrine with Raspberry Sauce
    Baked Banana with Cinnamon and Apple Cider
    Floating Islands with Raspberry Fruit Soup
    Melon Balls with Warm Ginger Sauce

MAINE CHANCE (Arizona)   91
        Hot Blueberry Cobbler / Baklava
        Raspberry Ice with Fresh Strawberries
        Frozen Vanilla Yogurt with Fresh Fruit / Fruit Soup

GURNEY'S INN RESORT AND SPA (New York)   97
        Chiffon Cake / Pots of Chocolate
        Banana-Strawberry Mousse / No Bake Pineapple Cheesecake

NORWICH INN AND SPA (Connecticut)   103
        Melba Meringues / Strawberry-Rhubarb Parfait
        Poached Pear with Raspberry Purée
        Oatmeal Raisin Cookies
        Connecticut Baked Apples with Spa Cream
        Honey Cinnamon Custard with Maple Syrup Sauce
        Pineapple Lime Sorbet

CAL-A-VIE (California)   111
        Mocha Parfait / Chocolate Swirl Pie / Orange Kiwi Sorbet
        Butternut Squash Flan / Fruit Mosaic with Sabayon Sauce

DORAL SATURNIA (Florida)   117
        Blueberry Apple Crisp / Orange Coffee Cake
        Tulip Cookies with Fruit Sorbet

THE HEARTLAND (Illinois)   121
        Maple Flan with Walnuts / Blueberry Nut Cake
        Frozen Jamoca Mousse / Date Nut Bar
        Frozen Orange Cream / Strawberry or Peach Crêpes
        Pumpkin Flan / Applesauce Carrot Cake
        Apple Strudel with Cinnamon Sauce
        Peanut Butter Granola Rolls
        Banana Cake with Lemon Cream Frosting
        Angel Food Cake with Puréed Pears

KING RANCH HEALTH SPA AND FITNESS RESORT (Canada)   135
    Chocolate Brownies / Cinnamon Date Coffee Cake
    Banana Crêpes with Orange Sauce

RANCHO LA PUERTA (Mexico)   139
    Frozen Lemon Roulade / Strawberry Shortcake
    Orange Yogurt Cream / Strawberries Grand Marnier
    Fruit Coulis (Purée)

JIMMY LESAGE'S NEW LIFE SPA (Vermont)   145
    Apple Crisp / Frozen Banana Mousse
    Blueberry Honey Cake / Tangy Banana Cheesecake

Alphabetical Index   151

Acknowledgments

Photography by Richard Allen.
Photo design consultant, Don Fernley.
Food styling by Rosemary Superville.
Editing by Nancy Kilpatrick.
Flowers donated by The Flower Centre in Toronto.
Tableware donated by Villeroy and Boch Ltd. in Toronto.
Tableware and housewares donated by Wares and Wares in Toronto.
Tableware donated by Junors in Toronto with a special thanks to
    Carmela Addonte Masterton.
Tableware donated by Grant's Fine China and Gifts in Toronto.
Materials donated by B. B. Bargoon's in Toronto.
Some of the desserts prepared for the photographs were produced by the
    Toronto Four Seasons "Inn on the Park" pastry chef, Sitram Sharma.

I have always loved preparing and testing excellent desserts, especially those with chocolate, butter, eggs, and cream. Mmmm! But whenever I had to taste diet desserts, I cringed at the thought—fruit prepared a thousand different ways, mixed with artificial sweetener, atop something which looked like dough.

In September of 1989, I was *enlightened* during a visit to the famous, and I might add, magnificent Canyon Ranch. Meal after meal, I enjoyed the lightest, tastiest, and richest desserts I could imagine, all low in calories, fat, and cholesterol. The challenge was there to pick up. How could I do it? Could I enlist the expertise of North America's greatest spas to produce the first collection of their recipes, tested and altered so that any one of these delectables could be successfully prepared in your kitchen?

Voilà! One year later, I present my choice of the twenty-one best spas on this continent and the secrets of their best light desserts. The spas share the goal of lowering fat and sugar in dessert recipes so that taste and texture are not compromised. Fat is reduced or substituted with other natural ingredients. These recipes will hopefully encourage you to take the further step of looking at your own dessert recipes. The truth is that you will be surprised to learn how much less sugar and fat your recipes can use without losing flavor and texture.

Every spa chef has been trained in pastry and now incorporates healthy, low calorie, low cholesterol ingredients in his/her dessert menus. And the creations are unbelievable. Cheesecakes taste better than those with many times the fat and calories. Mousses are creamier, without the whipping cream. Cakes are moister because of their natural liquids. And sorbets, frozen yogurts, and ice milk, lavished with natural flavors, can taste even better than ice cream. If you want to substitute sugar or fat products in the recipes, just refer to the page of substitutions, and like magic, any dessert will work.

Information provided about food products, garnishing techniques, and necessary equipment, as well as helpful hints in baking, should help make preparing these desserts a joyous and fruitful experience.

So indulge, enjoy, be guilt-free, and stay healthy with Spa Desserts!

Health professionals may argue about what constitutes a healthy diet, but the most agreed upon diet requires 55% of total calories to come from carbohydrates, 15% from protein, and no more than 30% from fat. North American and European diets tend to be much higher in fat and far lower in carbohydrates than is considered by many to be health enhancing.

According to the latest research, there appears to be a direct connection between what we eat and heart problems: in North America over 60 million people are affected by heart or blood vessel disease. Many heart problems are caused by fat and cholesterol narrowing arteries over a period of years. Blood cannot flow freely through these arteries, and this increases the chances of a heart attack or stroke occurring.

As well, there seems to be a connection between cancer (and, consequently, preventing cancer) and certain foods we eat. Research indicates that at least 35% of all cancers are related to diet. Scientists are proving that fat increases cancer risk, especially of the breast and colon, while fiber may actually prevent certain cancers of the stomach and colon from developing. To date there is no cancer-free diet, but some general guidelines and recommendations seem wise to follow.

Controlling the Risk of Heart Disease

Due to family or age, some factors contributing to heart disease may be uncontrollable. But many are within our control.

   a) Check blood pressure regularly.
   b) Check cholesterol regularly.
   c) Exercise at least three times a week.
   d) Stay at an ideal body weight.
   e) Keep alcohol consumption down to one drink or less per day.
   f) Eat a well-balanced diet, with 15% of calorie intake coming from protein, 30% from fat.
   g) Avoid smoking.
   h) Try to keep stress to a minimum.

Dietary Guidelines for Cancer Prevention

   a) Lower daily fat intake to no more than 30% of total calories.

b) Increase fiber in your diet.

c) Increase daily consumption of fruits and vegetables.

d) Reduce alcohol consumption to one or two drinks per day.

e) Reduce intake of smoked and salted foods.

f) Watch weight closely and keep it within a normal range.

Cholesterol: The Major Factor

Cholesterol runs through the bloodstream to the body's tissues. It is a necessary agent for making essential hormones and vitamin D, and for forming sheaths to insulate nerve fibers. But excessive cholesterol is a major concern. It creates a build-up of fatty deposits inside the arteries that over time will narrow them and reduce blood flow. The result can lead to a heart attack or stroke.

The typical North American diet is probably a factor in rising cholesterol levels. Statistics indicate that year after year death from arteriosclerosis is increasing.

Two carriers transport cholesterol:

1) High Density Lipoprotein (HDL)

This is a good cholesterol because it delivers excess cholesterol to the liver to be processed into other things that the body needs in order to function properly. The higher the HDL the better. HDL can be raised by exercising, not smoking, and maintaining an ideal body weight. Heredity, gender, and dietary factors also play a role in affecting HDL level.

2) Low Density Lipoprotein (LDL)

This is the bad cholesterol associated with heart disease which leads to excessive fatty deposits on the arteries, stopping the proper blood flow to the heart. It can be lowered by loss of excess weight and also by reducing the amount of dietary cholesterol consumed.

Saturated Fat

Saturated fat becomes solid at room temperature and hardens at body temperature. Found in meat, cheese, and butter, it is associated with an increase in blood cholesterol. Certain oils, such as coconut and palm oils, and other oils that have been hydrogenated (turned from liquid oil into a solid form), are very high in saturated fat.

Monounsaturated Fat

These fats stay liquid at room temperature and do not increase blood cholesterol. Examples are olive, peanut, and canola (rapeseed) oil.

Polyunsaturated Fat

These fats are found in sunflower, corn, soybean, and safflower oils and can reduce blood cholesterol. They should be used in their liquid form.

Desserts

Desserts have always been and still seem to be the most momentous part of any meal. They are the finale to a gala evening or a single family dinner. Most of us are hooked on desserts. The negative aspects of desserts have already been outlined (cholesterol and fat). But this does not mean we can no longer indulge our national taste for sweets. Desserts can still be eaten daily, provided we reduce portions and adapt ingredients to conform to healthier lifestyles.

Eating desserts lower in fat and sugar and higher in fiber seems to be the answer. The desserts in this book fit these criteria without compromising taste. At the end of each recipe in this book is a nutritional analysis of each dessert. The calculations are based on a single serving. And you can still use many of your old favorite dessert recipes, with these simple modifications:

a) Decrease the sugar called for or use sugar substitutes and taste for flavor. You will be surprised at how little sugar you can get away with.
b) Decrease the fat in the recipe. For example, substitute margarine for butter, yogurt for sour cream, and low-fat milk for cream. The dessert will taste lighter.
c) Increase fiber by substituting whole-wheat for all-purpose flour and using bran and wheat germ products.

Sugar

The average North American consumes approximately one and a half pounds of sugar a week. Sugar is hidden in many prepared foods. Extra sugar can cause weight gain. Sugar supplies some energy to our bodies but adds little in the way of nutrients.

In most recipes sugar content can be reduced by 50 to 75%, and the desserts will still taste delicious. Sugar is most necessary in cakes requiring a lot of volume, for example angel food cakes.

In order to decrease the sugar in your diet, try the following:

a) Reduce the sugar in your favorite dessert recipes by as much as half. You will be surprised by the excellent results. This will also help lower your desire for greater amounts of sugar.

b) Eat more fruit for dessert or prepare more fruit-based desserts.

c) Use unsweetened fruit coulis (purées) instead of sweet preserves.

d) Drink unsweetened fruit juices instead of sugared beverages.

e) Instead of fruit-flavored yogurts, try plain yogurt and add your own unsweetened fruit.

f) Flavors that give the illusion of sweetness are vanilla, cinnamon, and nutmeg, and small amounts of liqueur can be substituted for sugar. Use these while decreasing sugar.

g) Substitute equal carob for chocolate. Carob comes from a tree in the legume family. Inside the tree's hard brown pods are seeds that are crushed to make carob powder, which can be purchased in health food stores and some supermarkets.

Fat

Most North Americans get more than 40% of their daily calories from fat. Fat, like sugar, is hidden in many prepared foods. If the amount of fat we consume were reduced by half, we all would be slimmer and healthier.

The goal is not to remove all the fat from our diet so that food becomes bland and tasteless. Instead, be aware of where fat is hidden in foods and limit the amount consumed.

To lower the fat in your diet, try the following:

a) Substitute milk, buttermilk, and evaporated skim milk for cream.

b) Use yogurt instead of sour cream.

c) Use cottage cheese, ricotta cheese, or farmers' cheese in place of cream cheese.

d) In mousse, substitute beaten egg whites for whipped cream.

e) Use cookie crumb crusts instead of dough crusts, which have twice the fat.

f) Instead of ice cream have frozen yogurt, sherbet, or ice milk.

g) Try diet margarine, which has less fat than regular margarine, and whipped butter, which has less fat than regular butter.

h) Substitute whole milk for cream, except when the cream must be whipped.

i) Use a nonstick vegetable spray to coat fry pans and baking pans instead of butter.

Fiber

The average North American diet tends to be too low in fiber. Increasing fiber intake would have beneficial results. The way to add daily fiber is eat whole grain breads and cereals and more fruits and vegetables. These foods are generally lower in fat and calories but supply nutrition.

Research indicates that fiber may help lower cholesterol levels and also fight certain types of cancer, particularly cancer of the colon. Increase fiber in your diet by following these tips:

a) Add bran or wheat germ to muffins, cookies, and fruit dessert toppings.

b) Have at least four or five servings of fresh fruit and vegetables in your diet per day.

c) Eat fruits rather than drinking fruit juices.

d) Use whole wheat flour in dessert recipes. Substitute half the flour a recipe calls for with whole wheat flour.

Sweeteners

Saccharin-based sweeteners become bitter-tasting when heated. Aspartame sweeteners lose their sweetening power at the high temperatures required for baking. Therefore, neither is suitable for baking.

As substitutes for sugar:

a) The bulk granulated white or brown sweeteners look like and pour like sugar. One teaspoon sweetener equals one teaspoon sugar.

b) Packets—one packet of sweetener (Equal/Twin/saccharin) is equal to two teaspoons of sugar.

c) Tablets—one tablet sweetens the same as one teaspoon of sugar.

d) Liquid sweetener is concentrated; a quarter teaspoon is the same as one teaspoon sugar.

Sugar

Various spas use combinations of sugar, fructose, honey, or artificial sweeteners such as Equal, Twin, or saccharin. Naturally those that do not use sugar do not include it in their recipes. For substitution, please use the following information:

Fructose

This is a sweetener derived from the natural sugars in fruit, honey, and invert sugar and tends to be about one and a half times sweeter than sugar. It is more expensive than sugar, but price equals out because less is used. It can be found in supermarkets or health food shops. The following is a simple conversion chart:

$$1 \text{ cup sugar} = \tfrac{2}{3} \text{ cup fructose}$$
$$\tfrac{1}{2} \text{ cup sguar} = \tfrac{1}{3} \text{ cup fructose}$$
$$\tfrac{1}{4} \text{ cup sugar} = \tfrac{1}{6} \text{ cup fructose}$$
$$1 \text{ tsp. sugar} = \tfrac{2}{3} \text{ tsp. fructose}$$
$$1 \text{ tbsp. sugar} = \tfrac{2}{3} \text{ tbsp. fructose}$$

Brown Sugar

White sugar mixed with molasses to give it a brown color.
One cup sugar equals 1 cup brown sugar.

Powdered or Confectioners' Sugar

One cup sugar equals 2 cups icing sugar.

Fruit Sugar

One cup sugar equals $1\tfrac{1}{4}$ cups fruit sugar.

Honey *

One cup sugar equals $7/8$ cup honey.

Molasses *

One cup sugar equals $1 1/4$ cups molasses.

Corn Syrup *

One cup sugar equals 1 cup corn syrup.

*If you want to use these sweeteners in place of sugar, you should increase the flour or reduce the liquid in the recipe by $1/4$ cup.

Fat

Most spas do not use whipping cream, cream cheese, or sour cream. Following are some substitutes:

Cream

Heavy cream, whipping cream (35% fat), and crème fraiche are interchangeable. For whipped cream, all of these will work.

Light Cream

One cup equals $1/2$ cup whipping cream plus $1/2$ cup milk.
Do not substitute if *whipped* cream is called for.
For baking purposes:
One cup whipping cream equals $3/4$ cup milk plus $1/3$ cup butter.

Butter

One cup butter equals 1 cup margarine or 1 cup firm shortening.

Cream Cheese

Eight oz. cream cheese equals 8 oz. ricotta cheese or well-drained solid cottage cheese.

Buttermilk/Sour Cream/Unflavored Yogurt

In a recipe, sour cream, buttermilk, and yogurt can be substituted equally for one another.

Chocolate (Cocoa)

One oz. semi-sweet chocolate equals $1\frac{1}{2}$ tbsp. cocoa plus 1 tbsp. sugar and 2 tsp. butter.
Bittersweet, sweet, and semi-sweet chocolate can all be substituted.

Flour Products

One cup all-purpose flour equals 1 cup plus 2 tbsp. cake and pastry flour.
One cup all-purpose flour equals $\frac{7}{8}$ cup whole wheat flour.
In recipes calling for 1 cup all-purpose flour, substitute $\frac{1}{2}$ cup whole wheat flour plus $\frac{1}{2}$ cup all-purpose flour. Whole wheat makes a heavier, denser cake.

Baking Powder

One tsp. baking powder equals $\frac{1}{2}$ tsp. cream of tartar plus $\frac{1}{4}$ tsp. baking soda.

Other Food Substitutions

Coffee

One-half cup strong brewed coffee equals 2 tsp. instant coffee dissolved in $\frac{1}{2}$ cup hot water.

Lemon Juice

Juice of 1 lemon equals 2–3 tbsp. lemon juice.
Grated peel of 1 lemon equals 1–2 tsp. (5–10 mL) lemon peel. Lime and orange peel can be substituted.

Extracts

Try to use pure vanilla and almond extracts. They cost more, but the taste is well worth it.

High-altitude Baking

For baking purposes, high-altitude usually means over 3,000 feet. Two major problems here tend to be low humidity and excess sugar.

Tips for High-altitude Baking

a) Angel food and sponge cakes

The ratio of sugar to egg whites should be one-to-one. Thus 1½ cups sugar means 1½ cups egg whites.

b) Cakes with butter and quick breads

In these recipes use twice as much flour as sugar. Thus ½ cup sugar means 1 cup flour.

c) If you are over 5,000 feet, raise the oven temperature by 25°F.

d) Flour in cakes, muffins, and other desserts can be lessened by approximately 1½–3 tbsp. per recipe.

e) Major liquids (water, milk, juice) must be increased by 3–4 tbsp. for each cup of major liquid in recipe (do not increase extracts).

Please, no matter how competent a baker you are, read this brief section carefully. It is well worth the time.

Gelatin: one package equals one tablespoon. Gelatin should be dissolved by first covering with cold water, approximately ¼ cup. Let this rest one minute, then add ¼ cup hot water (or use liquids called for in recipe). Stir until melted.

Testing cakes for doneness: All cake recipes give approximate baking times because ovens, pans, and measurements differ. Nonstick pans can need as much as 25% less baking time. Therefore, ten minutes before the given recipe time is up, cakes should be tested by inserting a toothpick or tester into the middle. If wet, keep checking at five minute intervals. Sometimes a little bit of wetness in the middle yields a moister cake.

Cheesecakes: These differ from other cakes. Needing to be moist, a small portion of the center will remain loose after baking. To avoid cracks, loosen sides of cake with a knife to release the tension.

Preparing cake pans: The old technique to ensure that a cake will come easily out of its pan is to butter and flour the pan. If calories and fat are being watched, a nonstick vegetable spray will do the trick.

Whipping egg whites: Egg whites must be cold, fresh, and whipped in a clean, dry bowl in order to achieve the proper stiffness. If the bowl is wet or has any hint of foreign particles in it, the egg whites will never beat properly. Whip only until stiff peaks are reached. If whites will not whip, squeeze in a little lemon juice and continue whipping.

Fresh and frozen fruit purées (coulis): Usually 1½ cups of fresh fruit will yield approximately ¾ cup of purée, but always measure. When using frozen fruit, defrost and be sure to strain excess liquid before puréeing. If fruit is too tart, add a small amount of sweetener to taste.

Food processors: This machine can be used for mixing, creaming, and chopping. If a food processor is used to mix cakes or cookies, keep this in mind: after the flour has been added, use on-off motions to combine flour with other ingredients. Overbeating of flour results in a dry cake or cookie.

Loosening molds: To loosen contents, dip the bottom of the mold into a larger pan filled with hot water for five seconds. Invert onto serving dish. If unsuccessful, try another two to three seconds. Note that if the mold is kept in the water too long the ingredients will melt.

Helpful Hints to Achieve Perfect Results with the Following Recipes

Parchment paper: The greatest nonstick paper ever invented. When a recipe calls for this paper, butter and flour the paper or spray with nonstick vegetable spray to guarantee 100% success. Parchment paper can be bought in grocery stores or specialty cooking stores. It can also be reused.

Garnishes

You don't have to be an expert pastry chef to make your desserts attractive. Using basics can achieve spectacular results. (Always decorate if cake has cracked on top or looks unattractive after baking.)

Fresh fruit: The easiest, lowest calorie garnish and most beautiful decoration for any dessert is sliced fresh fruit.

Powdered sugar, cocoa, or carob powder. Simply sifting these ingredients over desserts works well. Use doilies to create beautiful patterns over a dessert. Individual designs can be cut out of paper and placed over cake top.

Strawberries: Decorate with sliced strawberries or cut stems off berries and stand up on cut edge with points facing up. Brush with clear jelly glaze and sprinkle with icing sugar.

Chocolate- or carob-glazed strawberries: Melt 3 oz. of chocolate or carob with 1/2 tsp. vegetable oil. Dip half of strawberry with fork or toothpick into chocolate or carob. Refrigerate on wax paper until hardened.

Jelly glazes: Use apple, strawberry, or red currant jelly to give fruit a sheen. Melt 2 tbsp. and brush over fruit.

Nuts: Toast in oven on cookie sheet at 450°F or in dry pot over high heat on stove top until golden brown. Grind into desired texture.

Frozen desserts: For ice milk and sorbets, ice-cream makers are irreplaceable. Follow the manufacturer's instructions. If such a machine is not on hand, simply pour sorbet or ice milk into metal pan, freeze until nearly solid, then purée and refreeze until ready to serve. Before serving, let sit at room temperature until softer.

Necessary and/or Helpful Equipment

Food processors: Great for grinding, beating, and mixing. Be sure to avoid overprocessing. Do not use for whipping egg whites or cream unless you have a special attachment. There are special attachments for whipping, slicing, grating, and juicing.

Electric beaters: Use for whipping, creaming, beating, or stirring. Gives greater volume to eggs, butter, and sugar.

Plastic squeeze bottles: Mustard or ketchup bottles are ideal for designing desserts filled with melted chocolate, yogurt, or fruit purées.

Springform pans: A deep round cake pan with removeable side. Small, medium, and large are all good to have on hand, plus 9″ size.

Large cake pans: 8″ to 9″ round pans are useful, especially when lined with parchment paper. A springform pan can replace a cake pan when greater depth is needed.

Bundt or tube pans: Useful for angel food cakes, pound cakes, and coffee cakes. A 10″ is the most common size. Always butter and flour or spray with nonstick vegetable spray.

Pie pans: A 9″ size is ideal. Those with removeable bottoms are best, and fluted edges add a decorative effect.

Decorative mold pans (2–4 cup): Good for mousse and sorbet desserts.

Jelly roll pans: Useful for sponge recipes. Line with buttered and floured parchment paper or spray with nonstick vegetable oil.

Bain-marie: Custard-type desserts or crustless cheesecakes at times require a bain-marie, or water bath. A larger pan than the baking dish is filled halfway with simmering water and the baking pan set into it for the baking time specified. This method ensures the dessert will remain creamy and smooth. Do not put a springform pan in a water bath—it will leak.

Pie plates and flan pans: The ones with removeable bottoms give the best visual results. The bottom lifts out to show a beautiful, free-standing pie or flan. The 9″ size seems to be the most practical.

Microwaves: I prefer to bake most desserts in a conventional oven. The microwave is great for melting chocolate (under the defrost element), toasting nuts, and reheating. Before baking in a microwave, refer to a microwave cookbook.

Convection ovens: Before baking desserts in this type of oven, be sure to refer to a convection oven cookbook.

Visionary in concept, warm and personal in nature, the Four Seasons Resort and
Club in Texas may provide the most comprehensive and accessible facilities
in the United States. A modern hotel with 315 elegant suites, a twenty-five-
thousand-square-foot state-of-the-art conference center, a fitness and sports
club, four restaurants, two cocktail lounges, and a luxury spa, Four Seasons
is located on four hundred acres of fresh, expansive Texas soil, only ten
minutes from downtown Dallas.

The Spa itself boasts unparalleled individual service and virtually every
important health and beauty treatment available. A personal consultation
through the Las Colinas Preventive Medicine Center located on the grounds
creates a unique health program consisting of conditioning, nutrition,
stress management, and health and beauty treatments. With thoughtful
amenities like a thick terry robe, personal hair-dryer, and twenty-four-hour-
a-day room service provided, guests feel like royalty.

Personal or studio classes in a variety of fitness activities are available
for all levels. Four Seasons offers racquetball, squash, indoor and outdoor
tennis, jogging on indoor and outdoor tracks, swimming in indoor and
outdoor pools, and golfing on the prestigious Tournament Players Course.

Full-body care includes Swedish and shiatsu massage; traditional water
therapies like sauna, steam, whirlpool, and cold plunges; outdoor sun deck;
Aromatherapy baths in pure, natural essential oils to rejuvenate skin and
senses; herbal wraps in linen sheets steeped in delicate herbs and oils;
loofah salt glow massages using a coarse mixture of salt to lift dead skin
cells and stimulate circulation; and complete hair and aesthetic services.

Executive Chef Berhard Muller, born in Germany, brings to the Four
Seasons' kitchens years of experience in European cooking. His à la carte
menu is lean in calories, cholesterol, and sodium. Desserts, while true to
his strict dietary standards, are abundant and rich in flavor. For example,
Coffee Chiffon Cake and Lemon Meringue Pie are delightful.

Lemon Meringue Pie

You'll never know the crust isn't there.
This lemony tart is great.

Preheat oven to 450°F
9″ pie plate or 6 small ovenproof dishes
Serves 6

Filling

1¼ cups water	Bring to a boil.
½ cup fructose *	
¼ cup lemon juice	
½ tsp. lemon zest	
¼ cup cornstarch	Dissolve, mix, and add to above
¾ cup water	lemon mixture. Cook until thick. Remove from heat.
1 tsp. margarine	Add and stir. Pour into pie plate or dishes. Cool.

Meringue

2 egg whites	Beat until soft peaks.
1 tbsp. fructose *	Add and beat until stiff. Pour over filling and bake just until brown, approximately 5 minutes.

Chill before eating.

*Fructose is a natural sweetener.
For substitutes see page 6.

Calories: 110

Protein: 1 g

Fat: 0.7 g

Cholesterol: 0 mg

Carbohydrates: 25 g

Sodium: 26 mg

Coffee Chiffon Cake

Coffee lovers will adore this unusual sponge cake.

Preheat oven to 325°F
10″ tube pan sprayed
Serves 16

2 cups cake flour **1 cup fructose *** **1 tbsp. baking powder** **½ tsp. salt**	Sift in large bowl.
½ cup oil **5 egg yolks** **¾ cup water** **3 tbsp. instant coffee** **(dissolved in a little** **hot water)**	Add to above and mix until smooth.
1 cup egg whites **(approx. 6–7)** **½ tsp. cream of tartar**	Beat in clean bowl until stiff.
¼ cup fructose *	Add to whites and beat another 30 seconds. Fold flour batter into whites carefully. Pour into pan and bake approx. 45–55 minutes or until tester comes out dry. Invert on rack to cool. Remove with knife around edges.

*Fructose is a natural sweetener.
For substitues see page 6.

Calories:	215
Protein:	4 g
Fat:	9 g
Cholesterol:	85 mg
Carbohydrates:	30 g
Sodium:	192 mg

Hot Spiced Apples
over Honey Vanilla Ice Cream

*This combination is like hot apple pie
with rich vanilla ice cream.*

Serves 6

Ice Cream

2 cups low-fat milk **¹/₈ tsp. vanilla** **3 tbsp. honey**	Boil in saucepan.
6 egg yolks	Mix in bowl and pour some hot milk into yolks, stir and pour back into milk. Stir over low heat and whip until thick enough to coat the back of a spoon. Do not let boil or mixture will curdle. Cool. Pour into ice-cream maker and freeze or pour into loaf tin. Freeze until nearly solid, purée, and refreeze until ready to serve.

Apple Mixture

3 apples	Peel, core, and slice thinly.
2 cups apple juice **¹/₄ tsp. cinnamon** **¹/₈ tsp. ginger (ground)** **¹/₈ tsp. nutmeg**	Mix in saucepan, add apples, and cook approx. 5 minutes.
2 tbsp. cornstarch	Dissolve in a little water, just enough to make a smooth sauce. Pour into apples and boil another minute. Remove from heat. Let cool slightly. Serve over ice cream.

Calories: 186

Protein: 6 g

Fat: 6 g

Cholesterol: 276 mg

Carbohydrates: 27 g

Sodium: 41 mg

Poached Pears
with Blueberry Yogurt Sauce

*The blueberry yogurt sauce with minty
poached pears is delicious.*

Preheat oven to 350°F
6 serving dishes
Serves 6

3 pears	Peel, core, and halve. Place in baking pan.
¼ cup frozen blueberries **1 sprig mint** **⅓ cup water**	Mix and spoon over pears. Bake for 30 minutes. Baste every 5 minutes, until pears are just tender. Cool pears in juice and invert. When cool, remove pears, place on serving dishes. Purée remaining syrup.
¼ cup low-fat yogurt	Add to syrup and blend. Place some on dishes, place pear on top.
banana slices	Place banana slices over top.

Calories:	63
Protein:	0.7 g
Fat:	0.4 g
Cholesterol:	0.3 mg
Carbohydrates:	15 g
Sodium:	5 mg

Honey Glazed Pineapple with Strawberries

Warm pineapple slices sautéed is an unusual dessert.

Serves 6

½ pineapple	Peel, remove core, and slice into thin wedges.
2 tbsp. honey **1 tsp. lime juice**	Sauté pineapple in honey and lime juice. Remove from heat. Place on platter.
¼ tsp. crushed peppercorns (optional)	Sprinkle over pineapple.
8 medium strawberries	Slice over pineapple. Serve warm.

Calories: 62

Protein: 0.4 g

Fat: 0.4 g

Cholesterol: 0 mg

Carbohydrates: 15 g

Sodium: 1 mg

canyon ranch®

It all began in 1978 when high-powered real estate developer Mel Zuckerman needed much more than a massage. Mel was fifty years old, had an ulcer, hypertension, was overweight, and had asthma. His father had just died of lung cancer. A sojourn to a California spa changed his life. In one month Mel lost thirty pounds, lowered his blood pressure, and learned to deal with his stress. He and wife Enid promptly bought the old "Double U" dude ranch located in the Santa Catalina Mountains near Tucson, opening the first coed health resort in America. A recent expansion to Massachusetts created Canyon Ranch in the Berkshires.

The two Canyon Ranch superspas work with the natural landscape. In the Southwest, amidst the earthy tones of sixty acres of desert sprouting giant saguaro cacti, adobe casitas (or "little houses") provide lodging for guests. In the Northeast mountains, the grand and lavish Bellefontaine, an historic 1897 mansion surrounded by 120 acres of woodland, is home to spa-ites.

Both spas offer overall health as well as unique programs geared to specific needs: arthritis, mind fitness, stop smoking, pre- and post-natal, overweight, underweight, and even executive health plans. Balancing mind, body, and spirit is where Canyon resorts excel. Current physical status and motivation are assessed by medical professionals and registered instructors, including stress-management counselors and natural health specialists, before a regimen is recommended. The various exercise classes are complemented by hiking, swimming, and racket sports. Pampering includes massages, saunas, steam, and unusual features like the eucalyptus inhalation room, cold dips, and nude sunbathing areas.

The Zuckermans turned to Jeanne Jones for menu preparation. A consultant specializing in light cuisine, Jones has prepared menus for some of the best restaurants and spas in North America. Author of seventeen medically acclaimed books on eating, her column "Cook it Light" appears in over 350 newspapers across the country. Her desserts are exceptional, and include a Pineapple Cheese Tart, Pumpkin Cheesecake, and a zingy Key Lime dessert delight.

Blueberry Cheesecake

*This cheesecake is creamy, light, and absolutely delicious,
especially with the sour cream topping.*

Preheat oven to 375°F
8″ cake pan or springform pan
Serves 16

Crust

2 tbsp. corn oil margarine *2 tbsp. water* *1 cup graham cracker crumbs*	Combine and pat in bottom of pan. Set aside.

Cheesecake

2 cups low-fat cottage cheese *¼ cup fructose** *2 tsp. vanilla extract* *1 tsp. lemon zest* *1 tsp. lemon juice*	Mix in food processor or blender until smooth. Pour into crust. Bake for 15 minutes. While baking, prepare topping.

Topping

1 cup sour cream *3 tbsp. fructose** *2 tsp. vanilla extract*	Combine and pour on top of baked cheesecake. Return to oven and bake 10 more minutes.
1 cup blueberries	Cool and decorate with berries.

*Fructose is a natural sweetener.
For substitutes see page 6.

Calories: 111

Protein: 4 g

Fat: 5 g

Cholesterol: 10 mg

Carbohydrates: 12 g

Sodium: 164 mg

Lemon Meringue Pie
Four Seasons Resort and Club,
Texas

*"Chokolate" Carob
Cake with Pastry Cream*
Canyon Ranch,
Arizona and Massachusetts

Zucchini Pineapple Bread
Canyon Ranch,
Arizona and Massachusetts

Banana Walnut Bread
Safety Harbor,
Florida

Fruit Blintzes
Canyon Ranch,
Arizona and Massachusetts

"Chokolate" Carob Cake with Pastry Cream

Better than most chocolate cakes you'll ever eat.
The pastry cream makes this cake heavenly.

Preheat oven to 350°F
Spray an 8″ cake pan or springform pan
  with nonstick vegetable coating
Serves 12

1 cup whole wheat flour **1 tsp. baking soda** **1 tsp. baking powder**	Mix in large bowl.
¼ cup crushed pineapple, **well-drained**	Gently mix into above. Set aside.
5 tbsp. water **3 tbsp. thawed, undiluted** **pineapple juice concentrate** **¼ cup corn oil margarine** **½ cup sifted carob powder** **(roasted)**	In saucepan over medium heat, combine and stir until margarine is melted and carob powder is dissolved. Cool. Transfer to food processor or blender.
¾ cup skim milk **2 tbsp. low-fat yogurt** **¼ cup fructose ***	Add to above carob mixture and blend. Add to whole wheat mixture and combine.
¼ cup sliced almonds	Add and mix gently. Pour into pan and bake for 20–25 minutes or until toothpick inserted in center comes out clean. Serve with pastry cream if desired.

Pastry Cream

1 cup ricotta cheese **1 tbsp. low-fat yogurt** **1 tbsp. fructose *** **½ tsp. vanilla**	Combine in food processor until smooth. Refrigerate before serving. Optional: decorate cake with cocoa or powdered sugar.

*Fructose is a natural sweetener.
For substitutes see page 6.

Calories: 226

Protein: 5 g

Fat: 8 g

Cholesterol: 7 mg

Carbohydrates: 35 g

Sodium: 249 mg

Lemon Frost

This frozen lemon dessert is one of Canyon Ranch's best.

6 small dishes
Serves 6

2 egg whites
$^1/_2$ cup water
$^1/_2$ cup low-fat milk powder

Beat in small bowl until soft peaks form. Be sure dry milk dissolves. Set aside.

2 egg yolks
$^1/_4$ cup fructose *
$^1/_4$ tsp. grated lemon peel
$^1/_8$ tsp. salt
$^1/_4$ cup lemon juice

In separate bowl beat together until fructose dissolves. Gradually beat into above egg white mixture. Spoon into dessert dishes and freeze approximately 2 hours.

**Garnish with mint sprigs
and lemon slices**

*Fructose is a natural sweetener. For substitutes see page 6.

Calories:	85
Protein:	4 g
Fat:	2 g
Cholesterol:	92 mg
Carbohydrates:	12 g
Sodium:	88 mg

Carrot Buttermilk Cake

Pineapple carrot cake is sensational with this delicate topping.

Preheat oven to 325°F
Spray 8″ baking pan or springform with
   nonstick vegetable coating
Serves 8

½ cup whole wheat flour *½ tsp. baking soda* *½ tsp. cinnamon*	Sift in large bowl. Set aside.
1 egg yolk *1 tbsp. corn oil* *4 tsp. buttermilk* *4 tsp. fructose* * *½ tsp. vanilla*	Combine in medium bowl. Add to flour mixture and stir until combined.
2 tsp. chopped walnuts *(preferably toasted)* *½ cup grated carrots* *¼ cup drained* *crushed pineapple*	Add to above and stir until combined. Set aside.
2 egg whites	Beat in bowl until small peaks form. Fold into batter and pour into pan. Bake 25–30 minutes or until center springs back. Remove and cool slightly.
4 tsp. fructose * *pinch baking soda* *½ tsp. corn oil margarine* *½ tsp. corn syrup* *2 tbsp. buttermilk*	For glaze, combine in saucepan and bring to a boil. Reduce heat and simmer on low for 5 minutes. Remove from heat.
½ tsp. vanilla	Add to sauce and blend. Poke holes in top of cake with a fork and pour glaze over warm cake.

Calories: 90

Protein: 3 g

Fat: 3 g

Cholesterol: 34 mg

Carbohydrates: 12 g

Sodium: 164 mg

*Fructose is a natural sweetener.
For substitutes see page 6.

23

Pumpkin Cheesecake

*A tall and dense cheesecake
contrasting lightness with spice.*

Preheat oven to 400°F
9″ springform pan
Serves 20

2 tsp. corn oil margarine	Spread over bottom and sides of pan.
¼ cup graham cracker crumbs	Pour into pan, shake, and rotate to cover bottom and sides. Set aside.

Cheesecake

2½ lbs. low-fat ricotta cheese **1 cup sugar** **1 egg white** **1 tsp. corn oil** **1 tsp. low-fat dry milk** **3 tsp. flour** **2 tsp. ground cinnamon** **½ tsp. ground cloves** **1 tsp. ground ginger** **¾ cup canned evaporated skim milk** **1 tbsp. vanilla extract** **1 (16 oz.) can mashed pumpkin**	Combine in food processor and blend until smooth. Pour into pan and bake 15 minutes. Reduce oven temperature to 275°F and bake an additional 1¼ hours. Turn off heat and leave cake in oven to cool. Refrigerate. Sprinkle with icing sugar.

Calories: 60

Protein: 0.2 g

Fat: 0.3 g

Cholesterol: 1.3 mg

Carbohydrates: 14 g

Sodium: 8 mg

Key Lime Dessert

A tangy lime dessert topped with browned meringue.

8 individual small dishes or
   1 quart soufflé dish
Serves 8

Filling

¾ cup fructose * *¼ cup cornstarch*	Combine in saucepan.
1½ cups water	Gradually stir into above. Bring to a boil over medium heat, stirring constantly. Continue boiling for 1 minute, until thickened. Remove from heat.
1 whole egg (at room temp.) *2 egg whites (at room temp.)*	In small bowl beat together until blended. Stirring constantly, slowly add half of above cornstarch mixture to egg mixture. Pour back into remaining cornstarch mixture and continue to cook one minute, stirring constantly. Remove from heat.
¼ cup lime juice *2 tsp. grated lime peel*	Add to above, mixing well. Pour into individual serving dishes or soufflé dish. Preheat oven to 400°F.

Meringue

2 egg whites *¼ tsp. cream of tartar*	Beat until stiff.
4 tsp. fructose *	Add 1 tsp. at a time to whites and continue beating. Spoon over dish(es). Bake 8–10 minutes until lightly browned.

Calories: 120

Protein: 3 g

Fat: 0.8 g

Cholesterol: 37 mg

Carbohydrates: 25 g

Sodium: 43 mg

*Fructose is a natural sweetener.
For substitutes see page 6.

Zucchini Pineapple Bread

*A great, light bread to accompany
any meal, any time of day.*

Preheat oven to 350°F
Spray a 9″ × 5″ loaf pan with nonstick
   vegetable coating or use traditional
   bread pan
Serves 16

1½ cups whole wheat flour
½ cup fructose *
½ tsp. baking soda
1 tsp. baking powder
¼ tsp. cinnamon
¼ tsp. nutmeg
¼ tsp. ground cloves

Combine in large bowl and mix
well. Set aside.

1 egg white
1 whole egg
3 tbsp. corn oil
1¼ cups grated zucchini,
well packed
1 tsp. vanilla extract
½ cup crushed pineapple,
well drained

In another bowl combine. Add
to dry ingredients and mix just
until combined. Pour into pan.
Bake approx. 45–55 minutes or
until a toothpick inserted near
the center comes out clean.
Remove loaf from pan and cool
on rack before slicing.

*Fructose is a natural sweetener.
For substitutes see page 6.

Calories:	103
Protein:	2 g
Fat:	3 g
Cholesterol:	18 mg
Carbohydrates:	16 g
Sodium:	9 mg

26

Fresh Fruit Sorbet

*Puréed frozen fruit is special
by itself or as an accompaniment
to many different desserts.*

Serves 6

**3 cups soft fresh fruit,
i.e., peaches/bananas/
berries/melons**

Peel, deseed, and freeze. Purée frozen fruit in a food processor and serve immediately.

Calories: 22

Protein: 0.7 g

Fat: 0.1 g

Cholesterol: 0 mg

Carbohydrates: 5 g

Sodium: 10 mg

Raisin Rice Pudding

A creamy rice pudding filled with plump raisins.

Preheat oven to 325°F
6 individual small dishes
   or 1 large soufflé dish
Serves 6

1¼ cups cooked brown rice
½ cup raisins

Combine and divide among small dishes or spread over larger dish.

1 cup low-fat milk
2 eggs
2 tbsp. fructose *
1½ tsp. cinnamon
1 tsp. vanilla extract

Combine in bowl and pour over rice in dish(es). Place dish(es) in larger pan filled with water (bain-marie). Bake approx. 25 minutes for small dishes and 40 minutes for larger dish, or until middle is set.

*Fructose is a natural sweetener. For substitutes see page 6.

Calories:	159
Protein:	5 g
Fat:	3 g
Cholesterol:	103 mg
Carbohydrates:	29 g
Sodium:	125 mg

Strawberries Romanoff

*Sliced strawberries folded into whipped milk
with a hint of orange liqueur.*

Place a bowl into freezer for
  1 hour before using
Serves 8

¾ tbsp. gelatin *2 tbsp. cool water*	Combine.
¼ cup boiling water	Add to above and stir until gelatin is completely dissolved. Set aside.
1 cup cold canned evaporated skim milk	Pour into chilled bowl, add gelatin mixture, and beat until soft peaks form, about 3–5 minutes.
*2 tbsp. fructose ** * *2 tsp. vanilla extract* *2 tbsp. Grand Marnier*	Add and continue beating until mixed thoroughly.
4 cups sliced strawberries	Fold into above. Spoon into 8 chilled dishes.

*Fructose is a natural sweetener.
For substitutes see page 6.

Calories:	75
Protein:	3 g
Fat:	1 g
Cholesterol:	5 mg
Carbohydrates:	13 g
Sodium:	18 mg

Fruit Blintzes

These delicate cheese and fruit–filled crêpes can be
served as a meal or as a light dessert.

Preheat oven to 350°F
Baking sheet
Serves 10–12

10–12 crêpes (pg. 31)

Filling

2 cups ricotta cheese
4 tsp. fructose *
or 6 tsp. sugar
¹/₂ tsp. cinnamon
2 tsp. vanilla extract
2 tsp. lemon juice

Combine and mix well.

¹/₄ cup raisins
1 cup sliced fresh fruit

Stir into above. Divide among
crêpes and roll. Place on baking
sheet and bake for 8 minutes.
Prepare sauce during the
baking.

Sauce

1 cup yogurt
1 tsp. vanilla extract
2 tbsp. apple juice
concentrate

Mix and spoon some sauce over
each blintz.

*Fructose is a natural sweetener.
For substitutes see page 6.

Calories:	96
Protein:	3 g
Fat:	1 g
Cholesterol:	40 mg
Carbohydrates:	40 g
Sodium:	90 mg

Crêpes

8″ fry pan lightly sprayed with
  nonstick vegetable spray
Makes approx. 10–12 crêpes

1 cup low-fat milk
1 egg
¾ cup whole wheat flour
⅛ tsp. salt

Combine all ingredients in a blender and blend until well mixed. Heat a nonstick crêpe or omelet pan until a drop of water will sizzle on it. Spoon 2 tablespoons batter into the hot pan and roll it from side to side, covering entire surface. When edges curl away from the sides of the pan, turn the crêpe over to lightly brown the other side. Repeat until all batter has been used.

Calories:	41
Protein:	2 g
Fat:	0.9 g
Cholesterol:	26 mg
Carbohydrates:	6 g
Sodium:	31 mg

For over a thousand years the Japanese have cultivated the art of personal service where needs are not simply fulfilled but anticipated as well. The Golden Door, considered by many to be the world's preeminent fitness spa, replicates the restorative care travelers receive at Japanese *honjin* inns, reconditioning occidental guests for their journey through life.

Back in 1958 Deborah Szekely created the Golden Door, a 177-acre retreat near Escondido, California. Closely set evergreens obscure this luxury resort that abounds in orchards and verdant hillsides, and even sports a charming brook with footbridge. The grounds, sculpted by a Japanese gardener, are immaculate, composed of ornamental trees and shrubs as well as a profusion of flowers. Low buildings of ochre with earthy roof tiles form guest lounges, dining room, studios, and a huge bathhouse. Interior and exterior are serenely decorated with Japanese antique art, even a three-hundred-year-old temple bell and a *koi* (ornamental carp) pond.

Regeneration in an environment of thoughtful service is the tradition of the Golden Door. Spa clothing is provided, including a Japanese kimono. At the Dragon Tree gym, equipped with state-of-the-art Hoggan Camstar Equipment, it's up at 6 A.M. for stretching and a morning walk, then return for breakfast in bed. Mornings and afternoons are filled with a variety of fitness classes, including the Golden Door da Vinci class, a heavy-duty aerobics session named for Leonardo da Vinci's theories of movement.

Steam room, sauna, Swiss hoses, and a fan-shaped therapy pool known as a Japanese tub combine with manicures, pedicures, scalp conditioning, brow waxing, facials, and masks.

Chef Tracy Pikhart Ritter, trained in classical French cooking, prefers low-sodium, low-fat menus, excluding red meat. From the Golden Door's "edible landscape" of organic fruits, vegetables, and herbs, she prepares and serves meals with Japanese flair, focusing on balancing flavors, textures, and colors with nutrition. All of the desserts are guaranteed pleasers— Chocolate Seashells, rich and creamy Raspberry Cheesecake, Pear Apple Croustade, and the light and lively Fresh Fruit Sorbets.

Raspberry Cheesecake

*This is a rich and creamy cheesecake
with raspberries throughout. It looks beautiful.*

Preheat oven to 350°F
8″ springform pan sprayed with
   nonstick vegetable spray
Serves 12

1 cup part skim ricotta cheese **1 cup low-fat cottage cheese** **¼ cup fructose* or** **⅓ cup sugar** **2 eggs** **⅓ cup low-fat yogurt** **½ tsp. vanilla** **1 tsp. finely grated lemon peel**	Purée until smooth and thick.
1 tbsp. flour **½ tbsp. cornstarch**	Beat into above.
1 cup fresh raspberries	Fold in carefully to above or save for decoration on top, after cake has baked. Pour into pan and bake for approx. 35 minutes or until toothpick inserted in middle comes out clean. Chill until cold and serve plain or with puréed raspberry sauce (page 106).

Calories: 91

Protein: 6 g

Fat: 3 g

Cholesterol: 57 mg

Carbohydrates: 9 g

Sodium: 109 mg

*Fructose is a natural sweetener.
For substitutes see page 6.

34

Chocolate Seashells

These soft chocolate cookies look wonderful when served with ice milk or with a small scoop of sorbet in between.

Preheat oven to 350°F
Madeleine cookie forms or other small
   cookie molds sprayed with nonstick
   vegetable spray
Makes 18 cookies

2 tbsp. honey **2 tbsp. apple juice concentrate** **1 tsp. vanilla**	Heat over gentle heat.
4 tbsp. cocoa powder	Whisk into above and stir until combined and thickened. Cool. Set aside.
1 tbsp. butter **7 tbsp. fructose* or** **9 tbsp. sugar**	Cream together.
1 egg	Add to butter mixture. Add above cocoa sauce and combine.
2 tsp. instant coffee powder **6 tbsp. apple juice**	Dissolve coffee in juice. Beat into above mixture.
¹/₂ cup flour **¹/₄ cup cocoa powder** **¹/₄ cup whole wheat flour** **¹/₂ tsp. baking soda**	Sift and fold carefully into above mixture until blended. Fill cookie forms about ²/₃ full. Bake approx. 12 minutes or until no longer wet. Cool. To create seashell appearance, slit cookie in half lengthwise, but do not cut right through. Prop open with a small ball of sorbet, ice milk, or frozen vanilla yogurt.
4 oz. sorbet, ice milk, or frozen vanilla yogurt (optional)	

*Fructose is a natural sweetener.
For substitutes see page 6.

Calories:	45
Protein:	1 g
Fat:	1 g
Cholesterol:	18 mg
Carbohydrates:	7 g
Sodium:	64 mg

Pear Apple Croustade (Roll)

Resembles a pear apple strudel.
Delicious when served warm.

Preheat oven to 375°F
1 baking sheet sprayed with nonstick
    vegetable spray
Serves 8

2 medium apples **1 medium pear**	Peel, core, and slice thinly.
⅓ cup ground cookie **crumbs (preferably almond)**	Add 2 tbsp. to above sliced fruit. Reserve the rest.
1 tbsp. fructose* or **1½ tbsp. sugar** **2 tbsp. flour** **1 pinch ground cloves** **¼ tsp. ground nutmeg** **1 tsp. cinnamon**	Add to above and toss well. Add remaining cookie crumbs.
4 sheets phyllo dough	Lay out one sheet over another and spray each sheet with vegetable spray. Spread fruit mixture over phyllo and roll carefully as in a jelly roll. Spray entire roll with vegetable spray.
	Bake approx. 25 minutes or until pastry is crisp and golden brown. Serve warm, sprinkled with powdered sugar.

*Fructose is a natural sweetener.
For substitutes see page 6.

Calories: 157

Protein: 2 g

Fat: 2 g

Cholesterol: 0 mg

Carbohydrates: 31 g

Sodium: 112 mg

Blueberry Apple Sorbet

Simple to prepare. Invent your own creations by substituting your favorite fruit and juices.

Serves 4

**1 cup puréed blueberries
(thaw if frozen)
1/2 cup apple juice**

Combine and freeze in ice-cream maker or pour into loaf tin and freeze until nearly solid. Chop into small chunks and purée until smooth. Refreeze for a short time before serving.

Calories:	34
Protein:	0.2 g
Fat:	0.2 g
Cholesterol:	0 mg
Carbohydrates:	8 g
Sodium:	3 mg

Strawberry Orange Sorbet

**1 cup puréed strawberries
(thaw if frozen)
1/2 cup orange juice**

Combine and follow instructions for Blueberry Apple Sorbet.

Calories:	24
Protein:	0.4 g
Fat:	0.1 g
Cholesterol:	0 mg
Carbohydrates:	6 g
Sodium:	0.6 mg

Orange Grand Marnier Sorbet

1½ cups orange juice
3 tbsp. Grand Marnier
approx. 1 tbsp. fructose*
(depending on sweetness
of oranges)

Combine and follow instructions for Blueberry Apple Sorbet.

*Fructose is a natural sweetener. For substitutes see page 6.

Calories: 63

Protein: 0.6 g

Fat: 0 g

Cholesterol: 0 mg

Carbohydrates: 12 g

Sodium: 1 mg

The exclusive Palm-Aire Resort and Spa might well be termed "Spa of the Stars." Favored by entertainment luminaries such as Liza Minnelli, Goldie Hawn, Joanne Woodward, and Paul Newman, this is the same health retreat that worked a miracle for Elizabeth Taylor.

Opened in 1971, this 1,500-acre mega-resort and country club is enormous. And popular. Situated on beautiful Pompano Beach, midway between Palm Beach and Miami, the facilities include a hotel and world class conference center, four dining rooms, and an adjacent spa.

Because of the variety of activities to choose from, Palm-Aire is perfect for couples whose interests differ. The surrounding area offers sightseeing, nightclubs, shopping, the Pompano Harness Track, deep-sea fishing excursions, and moonlit cruises.

Tennis, racquetball, squash, a half-mile Parcourse, swimming in a twenty-five-yard outdoor pool, five golf courses—four championship and one executive—and thirty-seven tennis courts are featured. Weight machines, aerobic exercise equipment, and freeweights are available. Classes range from low impact or aqua aerobics to stretch and the popular choreographed dance, all geared to individual fitness levels. Guests are tested and examined to determine body-fat composition, flexibility, and strength.

Palm-Aire excels in body treatments. Thalassotherapy, a newly introduced service, works in conjunction with other therapies: marine algae treatments (seaweed), Thalgomince (a natural body contouring mask), hydrotherapy tub baths, Frigithalgo (eliminates water and activates cutaneous circulation), Aromatherapy, and herbal body wraps. Guests luxuriate in Roman baths. Lip, body, and bikini waxing are available.

The gourmet menu, created by expert spa nutritionists and dieticians, permits guests to choose a calorie limit and compose their daily menu. Any of these scrumptious desserts are the perfect reward for energy well expended—Baked Alaska, Angel Food Strawberry Shortcake, or a divine Chocolate Angel Food Cake.

Angel Food Strawberry Shortcake

Whether you use this recipe with shortcake, sponge cake, or lady fingers, it will taste great with fresh berries and low-fat whipped cream topping.

Serves 6

Shortcake can be made with 12 oz. of store bought sponge cake, or by preparing shortcake recipe (page 141), or using 2 large lady finger cookies per person

Divide sponge cake into 6 pieces. Cut each piece in half to form a sandwich.

6 oz. low-fat dessert whipping cream mix (e.g., "Dream Whip")
1 cup ice water

Beat until soft peaks form. Place a heaping tsp. over one piece of sponge cake. Place second piece over topping. Reserve remainder of topping for garnish.

2 cups fresh cut strawberries

Place over top of cake. Serve with another dollop of topping on the side.

Calories:	240
Protein:	4 g
Fat:	5 g
Cholesterol:	0 mg
Carbohydrates:	46 g
Sodium:	105 mg

Baked Alaska

*What a great and simple way to
enjoy an old-time favorite.*

8–9″ springform pan
Serves 8

**12 oz. store bought sponge
cake, or follow shortcake
recipe on page 141**

Cut ¼″ thick slices to pan size
and place into bottom and sides
of pan. Save enough for top.
(Remainder can be frozen.)

**3 pints softened ice milk
(any 3 flavors desired)**

Spoon 1 pint ice milk over
sponge cake and repeat with the
other two flavors. Top ice milk
layers with sponge cake layer.
Ice milk should now be enclosed
with cake. Freeze until solid,
approx. 1½ hours.

Meringue*

Preheat oven to 450°F

**4 egg whites
sweeten with sweetener or
sugar to taste
(see sweeteners, page 6)**

Beat until stiff peaks form.
Remove sides of springform pan
and spoon meringue over cake.
Place in oven to brown for
approx. 5–10 minutes. Serve
immediately. Refreeze any
remainder.

*If desired, use low-fat whipped cream
dessert topping instead.

Calories:	254
Protein:	6 g
Fat:	9 g
Cholesterol:	35 mg
Carbohydrates:	35 g
Sodium:	136 mg

Chocolate Angel Food Cake

You have never tasted an angel food cake like this before.
The berries served make the cake moist and delicious.

Preheat oven to 375°F
10″ angel food tube pan lightly sprayed
   with nonstick vegetable spray
Serves 12

12 egg whites (room temp.)	Beat in large bowl until foamy.
¹/₂ tsp. cream of tartar	Add and beat until soft peaks form.
1¹/₃ cups sugar	Reserve ¹/₃ cup sugar. Add remaining 1 cup slowly, beating until stiff peaks form.
1 cup cake flour **¹/₄ cup cocoa**	Sift, together with remaining ¹/₃ cup sugar, into above. Fold in carefully.
¹/₂ tsp. almond extract **1 tsp. vanilla extract**	Add and fold in just until blended. Pour into pan and bake approx. 35–40 minutes until no longer wet inside. Invert cake, let cool, then remove by using a knife to loosen cake from pan.
Serve with sliced strawberries or strawberry purée	

Calories: 170

Protein: 4 g

Fat: 0.5 g

Cholesterol: 0 mg

Carbohydrates: 38 g

Sodium: 58 mg

Five Minute Chocolate Mousse

*Chocolate mousse has never been made
so quickly or tasted so good.*

4 individual dishes
Serves 4

**3 oz. low-fat dessert whipping
cream mix (e.g., "Dream Whip")
$^1/_2$ cup ice water
1 tbsp. cocoa**

Beat until soft peaks form.
Spoon into dishes.

Strawberries for garnish

Calories:	67
Protein:	0.7 g
Fat:	4 g
Cholesterol:	0 mg
Carbohydrates:	6 g
Sodium:	13 mg

Mixed Fruit Mousse

A creamy mousse that tastes like frozen fruit yogurt.

4 individual dishes
Serves 4

2 medium bananas	Wrap in foil and freeze for at least 2 hours. Cut into small pieces.
⅛ cup skim milk	Add to chopped bananas and purée just until little lumps are still evident.
1 cup frozen strawberries or blueberries **⅛ cup skim milk**	Add to above and purée until a creamy consistency is reached. Do not overblend. It is done when it has the appearance of ice cream. Freeze. Before serving soften slightly.
Fresh fruit to garnish	

Calories: 87
Protein: 1 g
Fat: 0.5 g
Cholesterol: 0.2 mg
Carbohydrates: 21 g
Sodium: 7 mg

Sheraton Bonaventure Resort and Spa offers a variety of fitness packages appealing to everyone. Fort Lauderdale is legendary and this resort makes use of its sunny, tropical environs. Guests choose the golf, tennis, or spa workout plan, but all plans include personal beauty and health treatments.

A combination hotel, spa, and convention center, the Bonaventure Resort is particularly geared to couples. Suites are modern and luxurious with all the amenities of a first-class hotel. Forty-three thousand square feet of spa facilities in tasteful gray and cranberry feature Keiser Cam II resistance equipment. Guests are encouraged to participate in a minimum of four organized fitness classes a day. These include aerobics and other workouts, levels predetermined by a detailed medical examination. In addition to walking, cycling, and swimming, riding at the fifty-one stall Saddle Club is an option (lessons available). The Resort even has a bowling alley and roller-skating rink. Racquetball, squash, twenty-four tennis courts, and two championship golf courses complete an unusually wide range of sports facilities.

Bonaventure provides separate spa pavilions for men and women. Sun decks, saunas, steam rooms, siesta rooms, whirlpools, hot and cold plunge pools, Swiss body-tone showers, and a variety of massages—including Swedish, shiatsu, aroma, and reflexology—are offered. Herbal wraps, loofah body buffs, facials, manicures, and pedicures (for men, too) treat guests to the ultimate in pampering.

Spa-ites receive a computerized nutrition profile. Body composition analysis is available. A spa menu of 900–1,200 calories a day combines with two quarts of Evian mineral water daily for weight loss and internal cleansing. Guests are given the freedom of choosing their own meals from menus that list caloric content of each item. Desserts are simply exquisite and special in the world of spas—luscious crêpes and a baked cinnamon fruit coupe.

Crêpes Suzette

The creamy orange filling in these crêpes
ensures a fabulous finale to any dinner.

Serves 6

6 crêpes (see page 31)

Filling

**4 tbsp. cottage cheese
(low-fat)
1 tbsp. low-fat milk**

Process until smooth. Spread each crêpe thinly with mixture.

**¹/₂ cup unsweetened
strawberry conserves
(jam) ***
**1¹/₂ tbsp. Grand Marnier
liqueur
1 tbsp. orange rind**

Combine in saucepan over low heat.

**2 tsp. cornstarch
¹/₂ cup orange juice**

Dissolve cornstarch in juice and add to conserve mixture. Slowly bring mixture to a boil, stirring frequently. When mixture thickens, remove from heat, spread 1 tbsp. of mixture over each crêpe, then roll up carefully. Place on serving dish. Spread 1 tbsp. of remaining strawberry mixture over crêpe.

**Strawberry and/or orange
slice for garnish**

Calories: 119

Protein: 4 g

Fat: 1 g

Cholesterol: 21 mg

Carbohydrates: 22 g

Sodium: 90 mg

---

*If unsweetened conserves cannot be obtained, use dietetic or sweetened conserves.

Blueberry Crêpes

*Blueberries and cheese always make
a great combination, especially
in a crêpe.*

Serves 6

6 crêpes (see page 31)

Filling

3 tbsp. cottage cheese **1 tbsp. low-fat milk**	Combine in food processor until smooth. Spread thinly over crêpes.
½ cup unsweetened blueberry conserves (jam) *	Heat in small saucepan.
2 tsp. cornstarch **⅓ cup apple juice**	Dissolve cornstarch in apple juice and add to blueberry conserves. Bring to a boil over medium heat, stirring frequently until mixture thickens. Spread approx. 1 tbsp. over each crêpe. Roll and place on serving dish. Spoon an additional tbsp. of blueberry mixture over each crêpe.

*Strawberry and mint leaf
for garnish if desired*

*If unsweetened conserves cannot be
obtained, substitute dietetic or sweet
conserves.

Calories:	99
Protein:	3 g
Fat:	1 g
Cholesterol:	21 mg
Carbohydrates:	19 g
Sodium:	81 mg

Baked Cinnamon Fruit Coupe

*Slivered almonds over baked fruit is a warm
dessert, especially during cooler months.*

6 individual wine glasses or serving dishes
Serves 6

Pinch of nutmeg *1 tsp. ground cinnamon* *2 apples, cored, peeled, sliced thin* *2 pears, cored, peeled, cubed* *½ cup seedless raisins* *2 cups unsweetened apple juice*	Combine in saucepan. Bring to a boil over medium heat. Reduce heat to simmer and cook 10 minutes, covered.
1 tbsp. cornstarch dissolved in ¼ cup cold water *1 banana, sliced*	Add to above. Cook 2–3 minutes until mixture thickens slightly. Spoon ½ cup of mixture into individual dishes.
2 tbsp. slivered almonds	Sprinkle with 1 tsp. almonds per glass. Serve warm.

Calories:	140
Protein:	1 g
Fat:	2 g
Cholesterol:	10 mg
Carbohydrates:	35 g
Sodium:	4 mg

The Pointe ®

The Pointe, with 1,840 suites, ten restaurants, golf courses, and riding and racquet clubs contained in three mountainside resorts each spanning over seven hundred acres of sun-splashed land in Phoenix, Arizona, is the largest all-suite company in the nation. These resorts, while perhaps not technically spas, are nevertheless included in this collection. The Pointe appeals to guests searching for spa amenities, facilities, and activities in a more relaxed atmosphere than the total concentration of a spa-only retreat.

Almost a village unto itself, The Pointe has properties at Squaw Peak, Tapatio Cliffs, and South Mountain. The architecture of the buildings can be described as Spanish Mediterranean. Resort interiors are resplendent with brass, marble, beveled glass, and grand staircases, the connection with old Mexico obvious. Guest suites are spacious and richly appointed.

Truly a total-destination resort, The Pointe offers a phenomenal range of activities: two desert golf courses; two hundred horses for breakfast trail rides and hayrides; thirty-three tennis courts with plexi-pave surfaces to cut glare; racquetball and squash courts; eighteen twenty-four-hour pools for midnight swims, with swim-up bars and underwater music; and two sports clubs providing full-service health spas. The sports clubs provide fitness assessments including nutrition consultation, exercise program recommendations, and medical diagnostic testing. Weight training systems, exercise machines, steam rooms, saunas, and scores of organized exercise classes from aerobics to specifics are available.

Highly skilled staff provide massage treatments in the form of Swedish, shiatsu, and sports-specific. The beauty salon works wonders after a day packed with excitement and stimulation. Guests can even have their nails done by one of the pools.

Meals at The Pointe range from casual to elegant dining. A smoothie bar and juice bar offering mineral water is available at the South Mountain in the multilevel sports club. The sports club dining lounge offers lighter dining, low on calories, to finish off an afternoon of working out. Savor these desserts: Tarte Tartin, Strawberry Cheese Tart, and the incredible Poached Pears in Chocolate Sauce.

Tarte Tartin

This classic dessert is always popular.

Preheat oven to 375°F
1 quart soufflé or baking dish sprayed with
    nonstick vegetable spray
Serves 8

5 medium apples	Peel, core, and slice thinly, place in bowl.
$^1/_3$ cup honey **$^1/_2$ tbsp. cinnamon**	Mix with apples. Pour into baking dish.
3–4 oz. puff pastry dough (store bought)	Roll out to circle of $^1/_8$″ thickness. Place over apples and bake approx. 25 minutes until golden brown. Invert onto large serving dish and serve warm.

Calories:	124
Protein:	0.5 g
Fat:	4 g
Cholesterol:	0 mg
Carbohydrates:	23 g
Sodium:	44 mg

Poached Pears in Chocolate Sauce

*Just a hint of chocolate makes
this pear dessert exceptional.*

6 individual dishes
Serves 6

6 small pears	Peel and leave stems intact. Brush with lemon juice to prevent discoloration.
1 1/2 cups pear nectar (or other fruit nectar)	Combine with pears over heat and simmer 20–25 minutes until cooked, but still firm. Remove pears from juice and chill. Reserve juice. When ready to serve, rapidly boil reserved juice until reduced to 1/4 cup.
1/4 cup semi-sweet chocolate chips	Add to reserved 1/4 cup juice and stir until melted and smooth.
1 tbsp. evaporated low-fat milk	Beat into sauce until smooth. Spoon some sauce onto dishes and place a chilled pear over top.

Calories:	167
Protein:	1 g
Fat:	3 g
Cholesterol:	0.3 mg
Carbohydrates:	37 g
Sodium:	7 mg

51

Strawberry Cheese Tart

Creamy ricotta cheese and yogurt topped with fresh berries
make a light and refreshing dessert.

1 prebaked 9″ pastry shell (page 69)
    or a store bought one
Serves 8

½ cup ricotta cheese *½ cup low-fat strawberry yogurt*	Mix just until smooth. Do not overmix. Pour into cooled baked crust.
4 cups fresh strawberries	Cut off stems and place stem ends down into filling.
¼ cup fruit jelly *½ tsp. water*	Melt and brush over strawberries.

Calories: 152

Protein: 3 g

Fat: 7 g

Cholesterol: 7 mg

Carbohydrates: 17 g

Sodium: 140 mg

Strawberry Cheese Tart
The Pointe,
Arizona

*Light and Lovely
Cheesecake*
Sonoma Mission Inn and Spa,
California

Chilled Mocha Mousse
Sonoma Mission Inn and Spa,
California

Raspberry Ice
Maine Chance,
Arizona

Strawberry Shortcake
Rancho La Puerta,
Mexico

**Individual Miniature
Cheesecakes**
Safety Harbor,
Florida

Oatmeal Maple Raisin Cookies

These maple-flavored cookies are soft, chewy, and delicious.

Preheat oven to 375°F
Spray baking sheet with
 nonstick vegetable spray
Makes approx. 30 cookies

¹/₂ cup flour
*¹/₄ cup fructose** *
¹/₂ tsp. baking soda
¹/₂ tsp. baking powder

Sift into bowl.

4 tbsp. margarine
1 egg
¹/₈ cup low-fat yogurt
¹/₂ tsp. maple extract

Blend into above and beat well.

1 cup rolled oats
¹/₄ cup raisins

Stir into above. Drop by heaping teaspoonfuls onto baking sheet. Bake for approx. 8–10 minutes until browned and no longer wet.

*Fructose is a natural sweetener. For substitutes see page 6.

Calories: 49

Protein: 0.9 g

Fat: 2 g

Cholesterol: 10 mg

Carbohydrates: 6 g

Sodium: 56 mg

Individual Sweet Apple Cakes

These unusual apple cakes are like indulging in your very own apple pie.

Preheat oven to 350°F
4 individual baking dishes sprayed with
   nonstick vegetable spray
Serves 4

2½ small apples	Peel, core, and slice apples.
¼ cup sugar **¼ tsp. cinnamon** **1 tsp. lemon juice**	Add to apples. Place in baking dishes. Bake for approx. 15 minutes. Remove from oven and raise oven temperature to 450°. Set aside.
½ cup cake flour **½ tsp. baking powder**	Combine.
1½ tbsp. margarine	Cut into flour mixture.
⅛ cup skim milk	Add to above flour mixture and form into a ball. Divide into four pieces, and roll each out to fit tops of baking dishes. After apples have cooled, place dough over apples in individual baking dishes. Cut slits for steam, bake for approx. 10–15 minutes until brown.
⅛ cup sugar **⅛ cup water**	Bring to a boil and pour over individual baked cakes.

Calories: 220

Protein: 1 g

Fat: 4 g

Cholesterol: 11 mg

Carbohydrates: 44 g

Sodium: 58 mg

Sonoma wine country near San Francisco boasts one of the loveliest spas. Sonoma Mission Inn has a long history, dating back to 1895 when hot water springs were discovered by the indigenous Indians on what had been sacred healing ground. It took nearly a century to perfect this romantic setting, with its medicinal mud and sparkling mineral water, into a peaceful resort.

Surrounded by groves of pine, palm, sycamore, and eucalyptus trees and splashes of colorful bougainvillea, the stucco-walled estate is an accurate replica of a California mission. Arcade and bell towers, a tiered marble fountain, white columns with glass walls and doorways, a two-story atrium with skylights, vine-covered gazebo—at Sonoma, exterior beauty alone soothes. Interior decor is a wash of pale shades, potted plants, fireplaces, and clean, open space. Guests are provided complimentary mineral water plus a bottle of Sonoma wine, the Inn's own label. Winery tours in Northern California are a must, and spa personnel eagerly arrange them.

Tennis, horseback riding, and swimming in the outdoor pool combine with Cam II Low Inertia Variable Resistance weight equipment to provide a variety of exercise. One special activity guests love to try is hot-air ballooning.

Marine salt scrubs, Fango clay body packs with seaweed, European hydrotherapy, Aromatherapy massage, wraps with Irish linen soaked in fragrant herbs, Swedish/Esalen massages, and baths that feature underwater massage are only a few of the features at this quintessential resort.

Executive Chef Charles Saunders is the recipient of several culinary awards, and the Inn's cuisine consistently receives accolades from leading restaurant critics. Saunders serves spa guests 800, 1,000, or 1,200 calories a day of what he calls "energy food," selected from the regular menu. Meals low in sodium and cholesterol are prepared from local fish and shellfish, farm-raised veal, free-range chickens, and organically grown vegetables, fruits, and berries. Cocoa Kisses, Light and Lovely Cheesecake, Berry Strudel with Papaya Sauce, and the classic Lady Fingers complete an evening of fine dining.

Cocoa Kisses

Soft, chewy chocolate meringues that are both exquisite and delectable.

Preheat oven to 250°F
Baking sheet sprayed with
   nonstick vegetable spray
Makes approx. 40 1" cookies

3 egg whites (room temp.)	Beat until soft peaks form.
1 cup sugar **1/8 tsp. salt**	Add gradually and beat until sugar is all incorporated and meringue is glossy and stiff.
1 tsp. vanilla	Add and blend.
3 tbsp. sifted cocoa **1/2 cup chopped pecans**	Fold into above until blended. Either drop by teaspoonfuls onto sheet or place in a pastry bag and squeeze kiss shapes. Bake until dry, approx. 60 minutes.

Calories: 35

Protein: 0.5 g

Fat: 1 g

Cholesterol: 0 mg

Carbohydrates: 6 g

Sodium: 8 mg

Vanilla Almond Snaps

*A nutty, crisp cookie that is
great with tea or coffee.*

Preheat oven to 275°F
Line cookie sheet with parchment paper
    sprayed with nonstick vegetable spray
Makes approx. 30 cookies

¾ cup blanched almonds **¼ tsp. salt** **¼ cup sugar**	Grind as fine as possible in food processor.
2 egg whites **⅛ cup sugar**	Beat into a firm meringue. Fold into above and combine until blended. Drop by teaspoonfuls onto cookie sheet and bake for approx. 25 minutes or until light brown. (Sprinkle with a few sliced almonds before baking if desired.)

Calories: 34

Protein: 0.9 g

Fat: 2 g

Cholesterol: 0 mg

Carbohydrates: 3 g

Sodium: 19 mg

57

Frozen Lemon Chiffon with Berry Sauce

Lemon lovers will devour this light,
airy, and tangy dessert.

Decorative mold pan or
    six individual dishes
Serves 6

2 tbsp. hot water **1 tsp. lemon zest**	Combine in cup and allow to steep for a few minutes. Strain and reserve lemon essence. Set aside.
¾ tbsp. gelatin **¼ cup lemon juice**	Dissolve gelatin in juice and heat slightly to completely dissolve. Set aside.
2 eggs **¼ cup sugar**	In separate bowl, beat until light and thick. Add gelatin and lemon essence mixture and blend.
¾ cup low-fat yogurt	Fold into above mixture. Pour into pan or individual dish. Freeze until set, approx. 1½ hours. Meanwhile make sauce.

Berry Sauce

½ pint strawberries, **blueberries, raspberries** **1 tbsp. fructose *** **2 tbsp. water** **2 tbsp. white wine (optional)**	Purée and strain out seeds. To serve, place frozen mold into pan of hot water for a few seconds. Invert and serve with sauce. (Allow dessert to sit out at room temperature for at least 10 minutes before serving.)

*Fructose is a natural sweetener.
For substitutes see page 6.

Calories: 190

Protein: 3 g

Fat: 2 g

Cholesterol: 80 mg

Carbohydrates: 35 g

Sodium: 30 mg

Chilled Mocha Mousse

*Chocolate and coffee fanatics will rave about
this lighter than light yet intensely flavored dessert.*

6 cup mold or soufflé dish
Serves 10

2 tbsp. cocoa **1½ tbsp. instant coffee** **½ cup boiling water**	Combine until all is dissolved.
½ cup cold water	Add to above and place in refrigerator to chill.
1 package (1 tbsp.) gelatin **¼ cup cold water**	Combine. Heat gently over stove or in microwave until dissolved.
3 tbsp. Kahlua or other coffee liqueur	Add to above gelatin mixture. Combine with chilled cocoa mixture until well blended.
1⅓ cups low-fat dry milk powder	Add to above and beat until smooth. Place entire mixture in freezer approx. 15 minutes to chill. Beat at high speed until mixture is very thick, approx. 5–8 minutes.
⅔ cup sugar	Gradually beat in sugar.
⅓ cup oil **2 tsp. lemon juice** **1 tsp. vanilla**	Beat into above until mixture is smooth. Pour into dish and chill at least 2 hours or until set. Sprinkle with powdered sugar, or decorate with carob-dipped strawberries (page 11).

Calories: 184

Protein: 4 g

Fat: 8 g

Cholesterol: 1 mg

Carbohydrates: 23 g

Sodium: 56 mg

Crisp Nut Cookies

This resembles the classic Jewish cookie mandelbrot.
Crisp and nutty, they are delicious.

Preheat oven to 350°F
Cookie sheet lightly sprayed with
   nonstick vegetable spray
Makes approx. 45 cookies

2 eggs **¾ cup sugar**	Blend well.
1 tsp. almond extract **2 tsp. vanilla extract** **¼ cup water** **6 tbsp. melted butter**	Add to above and blend well.
2½ cups flour **2¼ tsp. baking powder** **½ cup chopped nuts** **(pecans/almonds/pine nuts** **or combination)**	Add to above until dough can form a ball. Divide dough into 2 pieces. Shape into logs approx. 12 inches long. Place on cookie sheet and bake approx. 20 minutes. Remove from oven and cool 5 minutes. Slice at an angle approx. ½″ thick. Lay cookies on side and bake at 350°F until lightly browned, approx. 20 minutes.

Calories: 63

Protein: 1 g

Fat: 2 g

Cholesterol: 17 mg

Carbohydrates: 10 g

Sodium: 20 mg

Berry Strudel with Papaya Sauce

Mixed-berry strudel provides a nice change from apple.

Preheat oven to 400°F
Cookie sheet lightly sprayed with
   nonstick vegetable spray
Serves 8–10

18 oz. fresh or frozen fruit (combination of blueberries, strawberries, raspberries, blackberries, red currants)

(If using frozen fuit, thaw and drain off extra liquid.) Bring fruit to a low simmer for approx. 5–8 minutes. Do not overcook. Drain, reserve juice, and set fruit aside. Reduce juice by boiling until of a maple syrup consistency. Add back to fruit.

4 tsp. bread crumbs

Combine with above fruit mixture. Refrigerate until chilled. Meanwhile make sauce.

Sauce

dash of ginger to taste
⅓ cup water
1 tbsp. sugar
⅓ cup orange juice

Heat until boiling. Remove from heat.

1 papaya, peeled, seeded, and chopped

Add to above and purée. Set aside.

Assembly

4 sheets phyllo dough

2 tbsp. water
1 egg white
1 tsp. sugar

Combine in small bowl. Brush over each sheet of phyllo and spread chilled berry mixture over top. Roll up like a jelly roll. Place on baking sheet and bake approx. 15–20 minutes or until golden brown. Serve with papaya sauce.

Calories:	149
Protein:	3 g
Fat:	2 g
Cholesterol:	0 mg
Carbohydrates:	30 g
Sodium:	113 mg

Lady Fingers

An ever-popular soft cookie classic.

Preheat oven to 300°F
Line a cookie sheet with parchment
 paper lightly sprayed with nonstick
 vegetable spray
Makes approx. 25 cookies

4 egg whites	Beat until foamy.
⅓ cup sugar	Add and beat until stiff. Set aside.
4 egg yolks **1 tsp. vanilla** **½ tbsp. finely grated orange rind**	Beat until thick and lemon colored. Fold into above egg white mixture.
¾ cup sifted flour	Fold into above mixture just until combined. Place by heaping teaspoonfuls on sheet or pipe out of pastry tube 3″ fingers. Bake approx. 12–15 minutes or until light brown.

Calories: 41

Protein: 1 g

Fat: 1 g

Cholesterol: 48 mg

Carbohydrates: 6 g

Sodium: 12 mg

Light and Lovely Cheesecake

This light, cakelike cheesecake, topped with fresh raspberries, was featured in Chocolatier Magazine.

Preheat oven to 350°F
8″ springform lightly sprayed with
   nonstick vegetable spray
Serves 10

¼ cup graham cracker crumbs	Sprinkle over bottom of pan.
1½ lbs. ricotta cheese *⅓ cup sugar*	Combine until smooth.
3 large eggs	Add one at a time and combine until blended.
½ cup low-fat yogurt *1 tsp. vanilla extract* *1 tsp. finely grated lemon peel*	Add to above and blend well.
2 tbsp. cornstarch *1 tsp. baking powder*	Fold into above until combined. Pour into pan and bake approx. 50–55 minutes or until tester comes out clean, and cake is no longer loose. Chill.
Garnish and serve with 1 cup fresh raspberries and raspberry purée, if desired	

Calories: 183

Protein: 11 g

Fat: 8 g

Cholesterol: 113 mg

Carbohydrates: 16 g

Sodium: 134 mg

Raspberry Cream Sorbet

*Egg whites are the secret to making
this sorbet so creamy.*

Eight individual dishes
Serves 8

¾ cup sugar *¾ cup water*	Heat over medium heat until mixture sticks to the back of a mixing spoon, approx. 5 minutes. Cool slightly.
8 oz. fresh or frozen raspberries	Purée with cooled sugar mixture.
2 medium egg whites	Add to above, blend, and freeze in ice-cream maker or pour into loaf pan and freeze until nearly solid. Chop into small pieces, purée, then refreeze until ready to serve.
8 raspberries for garnish	

Calories:	90
Protein:	1 g
Fat:	0.1 g
Cholesterol:	0 mg
Carbohydrates:	22 g
Sodium:	13 mg

Built in 1926, Safety Harbor Spa and Fitness Center may not be the oldest spa in the United States, but it probably has the longest history. The spa sits over five distinct mineral springs, first discovered in the sixteenth century by Spanish explorer Hernando de Soto. He named them Espiritu Santo Springs—Springs of the Holy Spirit—and, because of their amazing rejuvenating powers, believed that the fountain of youth had been discovered.

Recently Safety Harbor Spa and Fitness Center was refurbished, modernizing the luxury resort and creating a playful, enchanting, and artistic ambience. Located on Old Tampa Bay near Florida's most popular attractions—Disney World, Cypress Gardens, Busch Gardens—and surrounded by pine forests, ancient oaks, and swaying palm trees, the expanded spa now includes a conference center with eighty-seat amphitheater and two boardrooms, catering to the executive crowd. Total health is the goal, with an emphasis on participation in one of thirty-five fitness classes, each low impact but effective, offered daily. As well as water volleyball, biking, jogging, indoor and outdoor pool swimming, outdoor basketball courts, weight training, tennis, and golf (both a 250-yard driving range and access to two eighteen-hole championship courses), guests can also try boxing training classes and box aerobics. Recently the spa established itself as a professional boxing training camp with top name pros in residence. This is surrounded by lush vegetation and exotic birds in a brilliant tropical setting.

Both steam rooms and saunas are a joy. But the *raison d'être* of this resort is luxuriating in the restorative natural mineral waters. Giving in to massages, facials, and herbal wraps is a prerequisite to evenings devoted to film, music, and live entertainment on the premises.

Guests select either a 900- to 1,200-calorie-a-day, low-fat, high–complex-carbohydrate, low-sodium menu, or order à la carte. Cooking demonstrations and take-home recipes are available. Desserts, while containing a minimum of fat, refuse to skimp on taste. Applesauce Spice Cake is a perennial favorite. Strawberry Kiwi Tart is luscious. And what could be cuter than Miniature Cheesecakes?

Individual Miniature Cheesecakes

The most creamy and delicious cheesecakes I have ever tasted.
Each is a perfect dessert for one person.

Preheat oven to 350°F
Line 10 muffin tins with
    muffin paper cups
Makes approx. 10 mini cheesecakes

½ lb. ricotta or low-fat
cream cheese
½ lb. cottage cheese
⅓ cup sugar

Blend until smooth.

1 medium egg

Add and blend.

½ tsp. cornstarch
¼ cup sour cream
⅛ tsp. vanilla extract

Add and blend until smooth. Pour into muffin cups and bake in a larger pan filled with water (bain-marie) for approx. 30–35 minutes or until tester comes out clean. Chill.

Decorate with fresh fruit
and glaze with 2 tbsp.
melted red currant jelly,
or serve with fruit purée

Calories:	107
Protein:	6 g
Fat:	4 g
Cholesterol:	43 mg
Carbohydrates:	11 g
Sodium:	131 mg

Applesauce Spice Cake

Applesauce, molasses, and spices create a moist, outstanding cake. Serve as a snack or dessert.

Preheat oven to 350°F
11"x13" baking pan sprayed with
   nonstick vegetable spray
Makes approx. 35 pieces

1½ cups applesauce
½ cup molasses
⅓ cup oil
6 tbsp. sugar

Combine well in bowl.

3 eggs

Add to above and beat well.

2¼ tsp. ginger
1½ tsp. cinnamon
½ tsp. cloves
¼ tsp. salt
1¼ tsp. baking soda
2¼ cups whole wheat flour

Add to above and mix just until blended. Pour into pan and bake approx. 20–25 minutes or until tester comes out dry. Sprinkle powdered sugar over top before serving.

Calories:	82
Protein:	1 g
Fat:	3 g
Cholesterol:	25 mg
Carbohydrates:	13 g
Sodium:	89 mg

Banana Walnut Bread

Banana bread at its best, moist and delicious.

Preheat oven to 375°F
Loaf pan sprayed with nonstick
   vegetable spray
Makes approx. 20 half-slices

2 bananas **8 tbsp. soft butter**	Beat until well blended.
$^1/_2$ cup sugar **1 egg** **1 egg white**	Add to above and beat until fluffy.
$^1/_3$ tsp. salt **$^2/_3$ tsp. baking soda** **$^1/_3$ cup chopped walnuts** **$^1/_4$ cup hot water** **1$^1/_3$ cups whole wheat flour**	Stir into above just until blended. Pour into pan and bake approx. 35–45 minutes or until tester comes out dry. (A few extra walnuts or sesame seeds can be placed over top of bread just before baking.)

Calories: 124

Protein: 2 g

Fat: 6 g

Cholesterol: 28 mg

Carbohydrates: 15 g

Sodium: 147 mg

Fresh Fruit Tart

A lovely dessert to serve that tastes as wonderful as it looks.

Preheat oven to 350°F
8″ tart pan with removable bottom
Serves 10

Crust

1 cup flour *1½ tbsp. sugar*	Mix together.
6 tbsp. cold margarine	Cut into above until mixture resembles oatmeal.
½ tsp. vanilla extract *3–4 tsp. cold water*	Add to above and toss just until dough comes together. Press into pan and chill 30 minutes. Meanwhile make custard.

Custard

1 cup skim milk	Heat slowly in saucepan over medium heat.
2 tbsp. sugar *½ tsp. vanilla* *1 tsp. lemon zest* *1 tsp. orange zest*	Add to milk and blend.
3 tsp. cornstarch *1 egg*	Combine until cornstarch is dissolved. Pour some of the hot milk mixture into cornstarch mixture, stir, and pour back into saucepan. Whisk constantly on medium heat until thickened. Chill. Bake crust for 20–25 minutes or until golden brown. Spread custard over crust.
Any combination of fruit	Slice and decorate custard with fruit. Glaze with 2 tbsp. of melted red currant jelly. Chill.

Calories: 220

Protein: 1 g

Fat: 4 g

Cholesterol: 11 mg

Carbohydrates: 44 g

Sodium: 58 mg

Bananas Flambé

An old classic that is simple to prepare and elegant to serve.

Frying pan sprayed with nonstick
    vegetable spray
Serves 6

3 bananas	Slice into approx. $1/4''$ pieces.
$1/2$ tsp. butter **$1 1/2$ tsp. brown sugar**	Add to pan and melt over medium-high heat. Add bananas to pan and cook until soft.
1 oz. banana liqueur	Add to above and ignite carefully. Serve immediately.

Calories: 86

Protein: 0.8 g

Fat: 0.8 g

Cholesterol: 0.9 mg

Carbohydrates: 20 g

Sodium: 4 mg

In a world of mass conformity, one spa is distinctive. Turnberry Isle Yacht and
Country Club's exclusive, luxurious spa is limited to just ten program guests
at any one time. The three-hundred-acre world-class resort located on the
private Aventura enclave along Florida's Gold Coast was founded by developer Don Soffer and is now owned jointly with the tasteful Rafael Group
(known for bringing elegance and artistry to their European and Asian
hotels).

The Turnberry Isle credo is simple: one person's needs are not neces-
sarily the needs of another. Detail is Turnberry Isle's specialty, uncompro-
mising old-world excellence the norm. Fitness and nutrition programs tai-
lored to the individual are implemented in refined surroundings. Pickled
wood, elegant silk fabrics, and imported marble-furnished suites 1,400
square feet and larger create the quintessential Mediterranean-style
ambience. Guests lack nothing, including fresh flowers, twenty-four-hour
room service, videocassette players, fruit baskets, and in-room wall safes.
The resort also offers limousine rentals and a helipad.

Spa residents are indulged and pampered, and every amenity is provided. Private exercise classes, stretching, water exercise, and aerobics
complement facilities that include swimming, twenty-four tennis courts, and
golfing on one of two Robert Trent Jones golf courses. Fitness clothing and
equipment are provided. Finnish sauna, Turkish steam baths, whirlpools,
Vitabath treatments, Swiss showers, massages, and body/herbal wraps all
soothe. Loofah salt-glow facials, manicures, pedicures, and a fresh hairstyle
all await Turnberry guests before an evening of dancing and entertainment
in one of five lounges.

Turnberry Isle also has five distinctive dining facilities—the Veranda,
the Grill, the Monaco Dining Room, the Sunset Room, and the Ocean Club
Grill. After a one-on-one consultation, the spa's nutritionist designs a personalized 1,200-calorie-a-day menu. Desserts are simple but flavorful and
served with a flair—Peanut Butter Cookies and the divine Chewy Cottage
Cheese Cookies round out fabulous spa cuisine.

Peanut Butter Cookies

Peanut butter lovers will be unable to control themselves when they taste these delicious balls.

Preheat oven to 350°F
Cookie sheet sprayed with nonstick
    vegetable spray
Makes approx. 40 cookies

⅓ cup soft margarine
½ cup peanut butter
1 egg
1 tsp. vanilla
½ cup brown sugar

Beat until light and fluffy.

½ cup flour
¾ tsp. baking soda
½ tsp. nutmeg
2 tbsp. sesame seeds

Stir into above just until combined. Form dough into 1″ balls.

Optional Coating

1 egg white
½ cup wheat germ

Dip balls into egg white and then roll in wheat germ. Place on cookie sheet and bake approx. 10–12 minutes.

Calories: 61

Protein: 2 g

Fat: 3 g

Cholesterol: 7 mg

Carbohydrates: 6 g

Sodium: 70 mg

Raisin Honey Cookies

Like a spice cookie, moist and chewy.

Preheat oven to 350°F
Baking sheet sprayed with
   nonstick vegetable spray
Makes approx. 36–40 cookies

¹/₂ cup water	Bring water to a boil.
1 cup raisins	Add, reduce heat, and simmer for 5 minutes. Drain and let cool.
¹/₂ cup oil *¹/₃ cup honey* *2 medium eggs* *¹/₂ tsp. vanilla*	Beat together in bowl and add raisins.
1¹/₂ cups whole wheat flour *¹/₂ tsp. baking powder* *¹/₈ tsp. nutmeg* *¹/₈ tsp. allspice* *¹/₈ tsp. ground cloves* *¹/₄ tsp. salt* *1 tsp. cinnamon* *¹/₂ cup chopped nuts* *¹/₄ cup wheat germ*	Fold into above and stir well. Drop batter by teaspoonfuls onto baking sheet. Bake approx. 8 minutes or until brown and no longer wet.

Calories:	83
Protein:	1 g
Fat:	5 g
Cholesterol:	16 mg
Carbohydrates:	9 g
Sodium:	18 mg

Chewy Cottage Cheese Cookies

These unusual cookies are creamy and chewy.
No one will guess they are made with cottage cheese.

Preheat oven to 350°F
2 baking sheets sprayed with
    nonstick vegetable spray
Makes approx. 36 cookies

¼ cup soft margarine *½ cup cottage cheese*	Beat until smooth.
3 tbsp. honey *⅓ cup sugar*	Add and beat until fluffy.
1 egg *1 tsp. vanilla*	Add and beat again.
1 cup whole wheat flour *¼ cup bran flakes* *¼ cup dry low-fat milk powder* *¼ cup toasted wheat germ* *2 tsp. baking powder* *½ tsp. cinnamon* *¼ tsp. salt* *¼ tsp. nutmeg* *½ cup raisins*	Stir into above until well combined. Place tablespoons of batter 2″ apart on sheets. Bake approx. 10–12 minutes.

Calories: 49

Protein: 1 g

Fat: 1 g

Cholesterol: 8 mg

Carbohydrates: 7 g

Sodium: 48 mg

 LA COSTA

Superspas are the latest development in the world of health and beauty resorts. One large and well-appointed establishment lies thirty miles north of San Diego. At the magnificent La Costa Hotel and Spa, nestled on four hundred rolling lush acres between the Pacific Ocean and the California foothills, guests are offered a seemingly endless choice of programs without any sacrifice in quality or personal service.

The La Costa experience includes 478 luxurious rooms, suites, and executives homes; separate health spas for men and women; fifty thousand square feet of conference center; eight dining facilities; three lounges; and even a 180-seat movie theater. Myriad fitness classes include early morning walks, cardiovascular workouts, aquathinics in the outdoor pool (balls and rhythm), and even the Costa Curves class. Eagle weights, Lifecycle Aerobic Trainers, and a computerized treadmill keep up the pace.

For relaxation, the ocean beach is minutes away. But the big draws for prominent figures from the worlds of entertainment, sports, finance, and the arts are two eighteen-hole PGA championship golf courses; a tennis program headed by the legendary Pancho Segura; and both indoor and outdoor swimming pools.

To actualize vibrant beauty, La Costa utilizes rock steam baths, saunas, Swiss showers, Roman pools, Jacuzzis, and private mineral whirlpool baths. Guests enjoy shiatsu and full body massages, loofah salt glow, herbal wraps, spot toning, and various types of facials in a darkened wooden room with fireplace.

La Costa also provides a lifestyle management program that includes medical analysis, lectures, goal setting, stress reduction, and balancing personal relationships. A separate spa-guests' dining room overlooks the gorgeous golf courses. Low sodium, fat, and sugar gourmet meals in ample portions of 1,000 calories a day are tasty, nourishing, and beautifully served. Peach Melba, La Costa Cheesecake with Strawberry Sauce, and an unusual and delicious Cinnamon Fig Cake are desserts to satisfy every sweet tooth.

Cinnamon Fig Cake

A moist, dense cake that, for a change, can also use dates or apricots. Great as a breakfast cake.

Preheat oven to 350°F
Bundt pan sprayed with
   nonstick vegetable spray
Serves approx. 20

1 cup chopped dried figs
1 apple, peeled, cored,
and sliced
1 cup raisins
1 egg
3 egg whites
½ cup fruit juice concentrate
(apple/orange or mixed)
1 tsp. vanilla extract
1 cup apple juice

Blend in food processor until smooth.

1 cup bread crumbs
(preferably whole wheat)
1 cup whole wheat flour
2 tsp. baking powder
1 tsp. cinnamon
½ tsp. nutmeg
¼ tsp. ground cloves

Combine well in bowl and add to above fig mixture just until combined. Pour into pan and bake approx. 35 minutes or until tester comes out clean. Sprinkle with powdered sugar.

Calories: 127

Protein: 3 g

Fat: 0.9 g

Cholesterol: 12 mg

Carbohydrates: 28 g

Sodium: 58 mg

Peach Melba

Contrasting colors make this a very beautiful dessert to serve.

4 serving dishes
Serves 4

2 peaches, peeled and cut in half	Place ¹⁄₂ peach in each dish.
¹⁄₂ cup raspberries, puréed and strained **1 tbsp. fruit juice concentrate (apple/orange, etc.)**	Mix and pour sauce over peaches.
1 egg white **1 tbsp. fructose ***	Beat until stiff. Place a spoonful over each pear.
Garnish with a fresh raspberry	

*Fructose is a natural sweetener. For substitutes see page 6.

Calories:	52
Protein:	1 g
Fat:	0.1 g
Cholesterol:	0 mg
Carbohydrates:	12 g
Sodium:	14 mg

La Costa Cheesecake with Strawberry Sauce

*A deliciously light cheesecake that looks spectacular
with the bright strawberry sauce.*

Preheat oven to 325°F
9″ pie pan
Serves 12

**2 cups low-fat cottage
cheese
3 tbsp. fructose***
**2 eggs
2 tbsp. lemon juice
2 tsp. vanilla extract**

Purée until smooth.

2 tbsp. low-fat milk powder

Add to above and combine just until mixed. Pour into pan and bake in water bath (bain-marie, larger pan filled with a little water) for approx. 30–35 minutes. Cool on rack. Chill. Serve with sauce.

Strawberry Sauce

**2 cups strawberries
1 banana**

Purée until smooth. Place approx. 2 tbsp. of sauce over each slice of cheesecake.

Garnish with whole strawberries (optional)

Calories:	84
Protein:	6 g
Fat:	2 g
Cholesterol:	53 mg
Carbohydrates:	9 g
Sodium:	168 mg

*Fructose is a natural sweetener.
For substitutes see page 6.

In the world of spas, one in particular seems synonymous with taste and class.

Midway between Dallas and Fort Worth is a luxury retreat known simply as The Greenhouse. It is here that fantasies are fulfilled.

Only thirty-nine women at a time experience the ultimate in personal service as the demands of the outside world fade, replaced by revitalization, renewal, and peace of mind.

Decor of lounges is restful colors and furniture of warm woods sculpted in the Queen Anne style. Individual suites surpass spaciousness. Adjacent bathrooms even include a bidet. The first night becomes memorable when there, on the pillow, lies a personalized credit card to the fabulous Neiman Marcus Department store. Once a week guests are limousined to Dallas. At Neiman Marcus coffee is served in a comfortable room while fashions that guests have expressed an interest in seeing are selected and then privately shown.

The routine of spa life itself is fairly organized, yet the focus is gentle discipline. A half-hour morning walk and another thirty minutes of stretching are followed by breakfast in bed, served on fine china and accompanied by a fresh rosebud in a Lennox vase. A series of exercise classes is held, plus tennis and sessions with resistance equipment. The sixty-foot indoor pool, with exercise bar down the center, is located in a room whose design gives this spa its name. Three stories overhead a vaulted skylight perfectly illuminates the marbled poolside and mezzanine terrace where white latticework, graceful arches, and potted palms and flowering plants abound.

Manicures, pedicures, hairstyling, facials, and makeup combine with daily Swedish massage, whirlpool, and thalassotherapy to revitalize and cleanse the system.

Executive Chef Michele Tezak, trained in classical French culinary techniques, presents sumptuous yet exquisite 850-calorie-a-day meals of natural fresh food. Fluffy Apricot Soufflé and Fruit Kabobs, both with raspberry sauce, are desserts as unusual and elegant as they sound. Strawberry Orange Buttermilk Sorbet is simply delicious.

Fluffy Apricot Soufflé
with Raspberry Sauce

*Small chunks of apricot create an unusual texture,
especially when combined with a fruit purée.*

Preheat oven to 300°F
2 quart soufflé dish sprayed with
   nonstick vegetable spray
Serves 6

Soufflé

8 oz. dried apricots **¼ cup water**	Cook until water evaporates (approx. 5 minutes). Purée.
¼ cup sugar	Add to purée until combined.
¼ tsp. almond extract	Add to purée and cool completely.
5 egg whites	In clean bowl, beat until stiff. Stir one third into cooled apricot mixture, then fold in the rest. Apricot pieces will still be evident. Quickly pour into dish. Bake in water bath (bain-marie, pan filled with water) in oven for 20 minutes. Turn oven down to 250°F and bake another 12 minutes or until light brown and no longer loose. Serve with raspberry sauce.

Sauce

1 cup fresh or frozen raspberries (or strawberries) **1 tsp. lemon juice** **½ ripe banana** **1 tbsp. fruit jam (any flavor)**	Purée until smooth. Strain to remove seeds.

Calories: 162

Protein: 2 g

Fat: 0.3 g

Cholesterol: 0 mg

Carbohydrates: 39 g

Sodium: 35 mg

Crunchy Apple Cobbler

*Crunchy granola over cinnamoned apples
makes a light dessert after any meal.*

Preheat oven to 375°F
8″ baking dish or
   6 individual baking dishes
Serves 6

3 large apples	Peel, quarter, and core. Cut into small pieces. Place in a bowl.
juice of ½ medium lemon	Pour juice in bowl with apples.
¾ tsp. ground cinnamon **2 tsp. honey** **1½ tbsp. melted margarine**	Add to apples and mix. Pour into dish and bake approx. 10 minutes.
¾ cup granola **(see following recipe)**	Pour over apples and bake 5–10 more minutes until golden brown. Serve hot.

Optional Topping

½ cup flour **2 tbsp. fructose* or** **3 tbsp. sugar** **¾ tsp. baking powder**	Mix together.
2 tbsp. margarine **1 tbsp. raisins** **1 tbsp. milk**	Add to above, cutting margarine into flour mixture until still coarse. Sprinkle over apples and bake approx. 15 minutes or until brown.

*Fructose is a natural sweetener.
For substitutes see page 6.

Calories: 148

Protein: 2 g

Fat: 7 g

Cholesterol: 0 mg

Carbohydrates: 21 g

Sodium: 38 mg

Homemade Crunchy Granola

Any combination of nuts or dried fruits can be used with guaranteed success. Keeps forever in a tight container.

Preheat oven to 250°F
Baking sheet sprayed with
   nonstick vegetable spray
Makes 2 cups—6 servings

1 cup rolled oats
⅓ cup chopped walnuts
⅓ cup unblanched almonds
2 tbsp. sunflower seeds
2 tbsp. sesame seeds
2 tbsp. pecans
pinch of ground cinnamon
1 tbsp. oil
3 tbsp. honey

Toss ingredients together in mixing bowl. Spread thinly on sheet and bake approx. 25 minutes, stirring often so that ingredients brown evenly. When golden and texture becomes crunchy, remove from heat and let cool.

Calories:	171
Protein:	4 g
Fat:	12 g
Cholesterol:	0 mg
Carbohydrates:	13 g
Sodium:	2 mg

Fruit Kabobs with Raspberry Sauce

Any fruit on hand will work for this dessert.
The sauce can also be puréed fruit.

4 individual serving dishes
4 skewers
Serves 4

Sauce

²/₃ cup fresh or frozen raspberries or strawberries (thawed)

Purée and strain through a sieve to remove seeds.

zest of one orange
1 tbsp. sugar
(or to taste)
1 tbsp. lemon juice

Add to above and mix. Set aside.

Fruit Kabobs

(Any combination of the following will work)
8 1″ cubes fresh pineapple
2 kiwis, peeled and cut into 8 pieces
8 orange segments
8 strawberries
8 slices starfruit

Put 2 pieces of each fruit on each skewer. Place some sauce on dishes and lay skewered fruit over sauce.

Calories:	114
Protein:	2 g
Fat:	0.7 g
Cholesterol:	0 mg
Carbohydrates:	28 g
Sodium:	6 mg

Strawberry Orange Buttermilk Sorbet

*This light fruit sorbet is delicious
in between or after any meal.*

Serves 6

¹/₂ cup water
2 cups buttermilk
2 tbsp. orange juice
¹/₂ cup honey
³/₄ cup puréed strawberries
(approx. 1¹/₂ cups fresh)
peel of ¹/₂ orange
(finely grated)

*¹/₂ strawberry or slice of
orange to garnish each
serving*

Purée and freeze in an ice
cream maker or pour into bowl
and freeze until nearly solid.
Break up with fork and purée
until creamy. Refreeze.

Calories:	99
Protein:	3 g
Fat:	0.2 g
Cholesterol:	1 mg
Carbohydrates:	22 g
Sodium:	43 mg

Chocolate Swirl Pie
Cal-a-Vie,
California

Banana Cake with
Lemon Cream Frosting
The Heartland,
Illinois

Chocolate Brownies
King Ranch,
Toronto

Date Nut Bar
The Heartland,
Illinois

Crunchy Apple Cobbler
The Greenhouse,
Arizona

Oatmeal Raisin Cookies
Norwich Inn and Spa,
Connecticut

*Peanut Butter
Granola Rolls*
The Heartland,
Illinois

*Crisp Nut Cookies
and Cocoa Kisses*
Sonoma Mission Inn and Spa,
California

When John and Ginny Lopis, designers of Florida's exclusive Doral Saturnia Spa and former directors of Arizona's Canyon Ranch Spa, recently opened the Spa at Topnotch on the grounds of the famous four-diamond, four-star resort in Vermont, it was expected that this facility would be exactly what the name states—top notch.

Here spa-goers are assured of finding something for everyone. The Lopises have integrated the spa into the surrounding Green Mountains near the quaint town of Stowe, incorporating existing outdoor facilities.

In a spacious, airy building, detailed wood interiors in shades of taupe, mauve, lavender, and spruce; fireplaces; bay windows; and walls of glass that expose spectacular panoramas bring the outdoors inside. Guest rooms are oversized and feature personal libraries and antiques plus landscaped garden views. Many outdoor activities are offered: mountain hikes, biking, fly fishing, canoe trips, English and Western horseback riding, golf, a heated pool, downhill and cross-country skiing for all levels, indoor and outdoor tennis, and swimming under a mountain waterfall. Indoors there is more tennis, swimming in a sixty-foot pool with adjacent Jacuzzi and cascading hydromassage waterfalls, coed saunas, and a bevy of modern exercise equipment. Fitness classes abound, including yoga and tae kwon do. Both men's and women's lounge and locker areas feature fireplaces, skylights, whirlpools, steam and sauna rooms. Herbal wraps, massage, reflexology, European hydrotherapy, facials, and body polish combine with makeup, hair, and nail treatments to insure that guests look as good as they feel. Two special features at Topnotch are the fitness library and an art studio, where guests explore inner creativity while learning relaxation.

Rated as one of America's top ten restaurants, Topnotch prescribes a "diet for life"—one that is realistic, rewarding, and takes into account age, activity level, lifestyle, and favorite foods. Meals, created by Spa chef Todd Weisz, are low in saturated fat, salt, and refined sugars, and high in fiber. As a finale, Baked Banana with Cinnamon and Apple Cider convinces anyone that healthy does not mean unimaginative.

Fruit Terrine with Raspberry Sauce

This is a spectacular dessert
because of the beautiful array of colors.
The bright sauce enhances the colors even more.

Loaf pan
Serves 6

2 medium oranges
¹/₂ pint strawberries
1 cup raspberries
1 cup blueberries

Remove skin and membranes from oranges and break into sections. Clean strawberries and cut into slices. Keep fruit separate and set aside.

Gelatin Syrup

1 tbsp. gelatin
1 cup apple juice or
any fruit juice
1 tbsp. orange liqueur
¹/₂ tsp. lemon zest

Combine all liquids in bowl. Sprinkle gelatin over top. Let sit for 3–4 minutes, then heat over water bath (bowl of hot water) until gelatin dissolves. Layer fruit in any order in pan. Between layers pour a small amount of gelatin syrup. Repeat until all fruit is layered, pressing down each layer. Work quickly so that the gelatin does not set. Pour remaining syrup over top layer of fruit and press firmly with a flat object. Refrigerate at least 1¹/₂ hours. Meanwhile make sauce.

Raspberry Sauce

1 pint raspberries
2 tbsp. sugar
¹/₂ tsp. lemon juice

Purée until smooth. Remove pan from refrigerator and place halfway up in warm water to loosen from sides. Invert onto serving platter, cut carefully into 6 slices. Pour some sauce over top of slices.

Calories: 122

Protein: 1 g

Fat: 0.5 g

Cholesterol: 0 mg

Carbohydrates: 30 g

Sodium: 6 mg

Baked Banana with Cinnamon and Apple Cider

The syrup produced while baking these bananas is so delicious you'll never want to eat plain bananas again.

Preheat oven to 350°F
Serves 2 (can be doubled)

1 ripe banana	Cut lengthwise in half, then cut in half again—4 pieces. Place 2 slices banana onto large piece of foil. Repeat with other 2 slices.
¼ tsp. lemon zest **½ tsp. lemon juice** **½ tsp. vanilla extract or 4″ vanilla bean** **6 tbsp. apple cider** **pinch cinnamon**	Combine and mix. Fold banana slices in foil making a tight seam. Leave one end open. Pour ½ of the liquid into each foil pocket and seal tightly. Bake for 7–10 minutes. Place on warm plate and serve immediately.

Calories: 84

Protein: 0.8 g

Fat: 0.4 g

Cholesterol: 0 mg

Carbohydrates: 20 g

Sodium: 1.6 mg

Floating Islands with Raspberry Fruit Soup

*Light egg whites together with this
tangy raspberry soup form a beautiful
and sophisticated dessert.*

4 decorative serving bowls
Serves 4

4 egg whites
2 tbsp. powdered sugar
1/2 tsp. cream of tartar
3/4 tsp. lemon extract
(optional)
pinch of salt

Whip until soft peaks form. Heat large saucepan of water until simmering. Shape egg white mixture into 4 egg forms and poach in water approx. 1 minute on each side. Remove and chill egg island forms. After chilling, pour off any excess liquid.

Soup

1/2 pint raspberries

Mash with a fork.

2 tbsp. red wine
1/2 tsp. lemon juice
1/2 cup orange juice
2 tsp. sugar

Add to above and mix until sugar is dissolved. Place 1/4 cup of soup in each bowl, and top with egg islands.

**Garnish with thinly sliced
orange rind or a sprinkle of
crushed nuts**

Calories: 80

Protein: 4 g

Fat: 0.1 g

Cholesterol: 0 mg

Carbohydrates: 15 g

Sodium: 65 mg

Melon Balls with Warm Ginger Sauce

*Warm gingery sauce over cool melon
balls can begin or end a meal.*

6 dessert plates
Serves 6

*1 small honeydew melon
2 small cantaloupes*

Scoop out insides with a melon
baller. Divide balls onto 6 plates
(approximately $\frac{1}{2}$ cup of melon).

Sauce

*2 tbsp. ginger finely diced or
$\frac{1}{2}$ tsp. ginger powder
2 cups orange juice
1 tbsp. raspberry or
red wine vinegar
$\frac{1}{2}$ tsp. lemon juice
1 tsp. honey*

Place in saucepan over medium
heat and reduce until you have
approx. $\frac{1}{2}$ cup. Keep warm until
ready to use. Spoon over fruit.
(Sauce can be reheated.)

Fresh mint for garnish

Calories:	109
Protein:	2 g
Fat:	0.5 g
Cholesterol:	0 mg
Carbohydrates:	26 g
Sodium:	19 mg

In 1932 legendary cosmetics genius Elizabeth Arden opened her summer home near Waterville, Maine, to friends, pampering and indulging them free of charge in one of this country's earliest spas. Eventually Miss Arden moved her women-only resort to Phoenix, turning it into a profit-making venture. Now Elizabeth Arden is gone, but her Maine Chance Fitness and Beauty Resort in Arizona, ranked as one of the top three full-service spas, is still *the* exclusive retreat for political dignitaries, entertainment personalities, and the quietly wealthy.

Miss Arden's 110 acre spa is hidden on an unmarked, rutted desert road, nestled at the base of Camelback Mountain. Passing through a white archway with iron gates, what first appears is a marvelous green lawn. Pink (Miss Arden's favorite color), blue, and yellow flowers in neat rows and a drive lined with whitewashed river rock lead to the main house. Furnishings create the ambience of a pleasant guest room in a private home: soft-pile wall-to-wall carpeting, floral chintz on a pastel background upholstery, plush chairs, writing desks, everything comfortable and soothing. Common areas are equally well-appointed, and the rooms feature paintings by Chagall, Magritte, and other artists.

The day begins with breakfast in bed. The tray is set with crisp white linen, silver cutlery, and fine porcelain. Then it's out to the pool. Exercise is encouraged and all levels are offered.

Because cosmetics was Miss Arden's specialty, beauty treatments at the spa excel. Guests receive daily massages, seaweed body wraps, as well as Ardena—body waxing that dates back to the original facility in New England and is composed of a body wrap in nine pounds of hot wax.

Harris Golden has been executive chef at Maine Chance for nearly two decades. He favors a nutritionally balanced diet in moderation. As author of *Golden's Kitchen: The Artistry of Cooking and Dining on the Light Side,* his light, lively gourmet cuisine is nearly mythic. When it comes to desserts, Golden excels. Hot Blueberry Cobbler, Raspberry Ice with Fresh Strawberries, and a luscious Baklava surprise and please.

Hot Blueberry Cobbler

*A hot and decadent cobbler that stands alone
or can be served with honey yogurt.*

Preheat oven to 350°F
9″ baking pan or
    8 individual baking dishes
Serves 8

2 pints blueberries
2½ tbsp. sugar
1 tsp. grated lemon rind
⅓ cup water

Combine in saucepan and bring to boil. Simmer for 2 minutes. Meanwhile prepare the following.

4 tbsp. soft butter
½ cup whole wheat flour
½ cup rolled oats
¼ cup brown sugar
¼ tsp. cinnamon
⅛ tsp. almond extract

Combine in bowl until mixture is crumbly. Transfer blueberry mixture to baking pan or dishes, and sprinkle rolled oat mixture over top. Bake about 30 minutes until browned. Serve with honey yogurt or frozen vanilla yogurt (page 95) if desired.

Honey Yogurt

2 cups plain yogurt
honey
(just enough to sweeten)

Combine.

Calories:	117
Protein:	2 g
Fat:	7 g
Cholesterol:	15 mg
Carbohydrates:	28 g
Sodium:	67 mg

Baklava

It would be difficult returning to honey-heavy baklava after trying this uniquely nutty version.

Preheat oven to 400°F
Lightly oiled cookie sheet
Makes 16 pieces

½ cup chopped pecans
½ cup chopped pistachio nuts
½ cup sesame seeds
¼ cup honey
1¼ tsp. lemon juice
1¼ tsp. cinnamon

Combine well in bowl.

6 sheets phyllo dough

Cut each sheet into 5"x5" pieces, totaling 32 pieces. Using 2 pieces for each baklava, spread approx. 1 tbsp. of above nut mixture in center of each piece of phyllo dough. Bring corners of dough together and pinch above nut mixture to seal. Place on cookie sheet and bake approx. 10 minutes or until golden brown. Set aside. Serve warm with the following fruit sauce.

Calories: 187

Protein: 5 g

Fat: 8 g

Cholesterol: 0 mg

Carbohydrates: 39 g

Sodium: 145 mg

Fruit Sauce

½ cup orange juice
½ cup apple juice
½ cup honey
3 small apples, peeled, cored, and cut into wedges

Combine in saucepan and cook until apples are tender (5–10 minutes).

powdered sugar and cinnamon for garnish

Raspberry Ice with Fresh Strawberries

If raspberries are not on hand, use any fruit.
Great complement to other desserts,
or simply enjoy it by itself.

6 individual serving dishes
Serves 6

2 pints fresh raspberries	Purée in blender or food processor and strain out seeds through a sieve.
Honey to taste	Add enough for desired sweetness. Freeze in ice-cream maker or pour into bowl and freeze until nearly solid. Purée in food processor and refreeze.
6 tbsp. yogurt **6 large strawberries**	Place a dollup of yogurt and one strawberry on each serving.

Calories: 60

Protein: 1 g

Fat: 0.4 g

Cholesterol: 0.5 mg

Carbohydrates: 14 g

Sodium: 10 mg

Frozen Vanilla Yogurt with Fresh Fruit

*So rich and smooth it is hard to differentiate
from vanilla ice cream.
Use as a side dish with hot baked desserts.*

Serves 10

**2 eggs
³/₄ cup brown sugar
1 cup 2% milk**

In saucepan over medium-low heat beat together with a whisk, stirring constantly until thick (approx. 5 minutes). Do not let boil, or eggs will curdle. Remove from heat. Cool.

**3 cups plain yogurt
2 tsp. vanilla extract**

Beat into above. Freeze in ice-cream maker or freeze in loaf tin until nearly solid, then purée or beat until creamy. Refreeze. Serve with following fruit.

Fruit

**2 pints blueberries
4 kiwis
2 bananas**

Place in large oval dish. Serve frozen yogurt alongside fruit.

Calories:	207
Protein:	5 g
Fat:	3 g
Cholesterol:	64 mg
Carbohydrates:	42 g
Sodium:	63 mg

Fruit Soup

Great to begin or finish a meal. Cool and refreshing.
Experiment with different combinations of fruit.

8 individual serving dishes
Serves 8

1½ cups apple juice
1½ cups orange juice
½ cup diced honeydew melon
½ cup raspberries
½ cup cut peaches,
mangoes, or papayas

Purée until smooth. Pour into a large bowl.

1 cup diced honeydew melon
1 cup cut peaches,
mangoes, or papayas
1 cup blueberries
1 cup seedless grapes
1 small lime cut into very
thin slices

Add remaining fruit to above juice mixture. Chill well.

½ cup egg whites
(approx. 3 whites)
1½ tbsp. sugar

Just before serving, beat until soft peaks form. Pour chilled fruit soup in dishes and place a dollop of meringue over top.

Calories: 135

Protein: 4 g

Fat: 0.4 g

Cholesterol: 0 mg

Carbohydrates: 30 g

Sodium: 45 mg

Gurney's Inn

East Coasters love the seashore, and perhaps no American has more faith in the healing properties of the Atlantic Ocean than Nick Monte. Keeper of Gurney's Inn for thirty-four years, Monte added a spa in 1979 to the Montauk, Long Island resort.

Romantically located on a strip of sandy beach, a complex of buildings is set against solitary dunes and craggy boulders. Rooms with the rustic charm of New England have private balconies opening onto the timeless ocean.

Guests come to Gurney's for many reasons, but it is the transformation worked by the waters here that most entices. A near Olympic-size indoor heated seawater swimming pool is one of the few around. Day begins with a brisk early-morning walk on the beach—the firming obtained from sand-walking is astonishing. Land-bound workouts include aerobics, calisthenics, isometrics, yoga, weight and exercise equipment, a challenging obstacle course, and a special program for worn-out executives.

Body treatments are extensive and feature seawater therapies available nowhere else in the United States. There are Russian steam rooms; thalassotherapy tubs of seawater; Parafango, a medicinal mud from hot springs in Battaglia, Italy; a unique wrap of concentrated seaweed preparation imported from the coast of Brittany, France; marine phyto therapy; Vichy-style hydrotherapy; sea-salt glow rubs using loofah and salt from the Dead Sea; Norwegian rubs with natural sponges from Greece; mirrored Roman baths fed with seawater; and a selection of massages—Swedish, shiatsu, polarity, crania sacral therapy, reflexology, neuromuscular repatterning technique, Trager bodywork, antitension therapy, biofeedback, and hydro-relaxation. Gurney's deserves its international reputation.

The spa cuisine is excellent, and guests choose their daily minimum 800-calorie meals from a large selection. High fiber, low fat and cholesterol foods with little salt and sugar and no MSG are the norm. Desserts are exotic: No Bake Pineapple Cheesecake, Individual Pots of Chocolate, and a Chiffon Cake as delicate as ocean spray.

Chiffon Cake

This light and airy dessert resembles sponge cake.
Fresh fruit served alongside is an extra treat.

Preheat oven to 350°F
9″ springform pan sprayed with
   nonstick vegetable spray
Serves 10

1 cup cake flour
¹/₂ cup sugar
1¹/₂ tsp. baking powder

Sift in bowl. Set aside.

2 medium egg whites
3 medium whole eggs
¹/₃ cup water
¹/₂ tsp. vanilla
1 tsp. grated lemon peel
1 tsp. grated orange peel

Mix in another bowl until combined, then slowly add to above dry ingredients. Mix until well combined. Set aside.

¹/₂ cup egg whites
(approx. 3 egg whites)
¹/₄ tsp. cream of tartar

In clean bowl beat until stiff, then gently fold into above mixture. Pour into pan and bake approx. 25–30 minutes or until tester comes out clean.

Fresh sliced fruit for garnish

Calories:	143
Protein:	5 g
Fat:	2 g
Cholesterol:	90 mg
Carbohydrates:	26 g
Sodium:	56 mg

Pots of Chocolate

*Ricotta cheese and cocoa combine beautifully
to make this an old-fashioned favorite.*

6 individual dishes
   or champagne glasses
Serves 6

1 large egg *³/₄ tbsp. gelatin* *1 tbsp. cold water*	Blend until combined and gelatin softens, approx. 1 minute.
1 cup boiling water	Add and blend until gelatin is dissolved.
1 tsp. instant coffee powder *½ cup ricotta cheese (low-fat)* *½ cup skim milk* *2½ tbsp. cocoa powder* *¼ cup sugar or* *5 packages sweetener*	Add and purée until smooth. Pour into dishes and chill at least 2 hours.
Strawberries for garnish	

Calories:	102
Protein:	5 g
Fat:	3 g
Cholesterol:	57 mg
Carbohydrates:	14 g
Sodium:	49 mg

Banana-Strawberry Mousse

Frozen and puréed bananas, strawberries, and orange juice—tastes like a marvelous ice cream.

6 individual dishes or
champagne glasses
Serves 6

1 tbsp. gelatin
¹/₂ cup cold water

Combine in saucepan. Let sit for 1 minute. Heat gently until gelatin dissolves. Remove from heat. Pour into blender.

3 small ripe bananas
1 cup orange juice
1 cup strawberries
6 tbsp. lemon juice

Add to above and purée until smooth. Pour into dishes and chill approx. 2 hours.

Strawberry or orange slices
for garnish

Calories:	82
Protein:	2 g
Fat:	0.4 g
Cholesterol:	0 mg
Carbohydrates:	19 g
Sodium:	5 mg

No Bake Pineapple Cheesecake

*Pineapple and creamy ricotta cheese make
a light and simple cheesecake.*

8″–9″ pie or springform pan sprayed with
   nonstick vegetable spray
Serves 12

¼ cup graham cracker crumbs	Sprinkle on sides and bottom of pan.
1 8 oz. can crushed pineapple in its own juice	Drain 3 tbsp. pineapple juice into a bowl. Set drained pineapple aside.
1 tbsp. gelatin *¼ cup boiling water*	Combine, let stand until dissolved, and add to above juice. Place in blender or food processor.
16 oz. ricotta cheese *5 packets sweetener or* *¼ cup sugar or other equivalent sweetener* *1 tsp. vanilla extract* *crushed pineapple from above* *1 tsp. cinnamon*	Add and blend until mixture is smooth. Pour into pan and chill approx. 2 hours, until set.
Decorate with fresh sliced fruit	

Calories:	88
Protein:	5 g
Fat:	3 g
Cholesterol:	12 mg
Carbohydrates:	6 g
Sodium:	52 mg

Edward J. Safdie, real estate magnate and designer of such luxury spas as Sonoma Mission Inn, The Greenhouse, and the California Terrace and Spa, has done it again. Nestled in the wooded Connecticut countryside on a twenty-five-acre estate, the Norwich Inn and Spa offers the ultimate sybaritic vacation. Far from the madding city, Safdie manages to blend historical New England and the country feel of English nobility in a spa limited to sixty-five indulged and pampered guests.

Rooms in this luxurious stately red brick country resort are awash with country prints. Step stools beside raised four-poster colonial beds of striped pine are the order of the day. The antique-laden atmosphere in the public areas of the Inn makes them luxurious and stylish. The spa building is a triumph of neo-Roman architecture. In these welcoming, light-drenched rooms with cool, sand-toned backdrops, fitness and beauty transformations occur.

Exercise classes are small, the approach intimate and personal. Lifecycles, rowing, and trainer-supervised Nautilus machines emphasize individual development. Tennis and golf are available. But the focal point of the spa is a gorgeous Etruscan-style indoor ceramic pool, tiled in white, blue, and green. Guests float and dream away tension under the twenty-five-foot cathedral ceiling.

Saunas, hydrotherapy, and steam treatments are available, including thalassotherapy to stimulate circulation and rid the body of toxins. Cellulite massage and a tanning salon are included. A round of facials and other beauty treatments insures the ultimate in toned sleekness.

An eclectic cuisine, internationally inspired, means tasty as well as balanced and calorie-conscious meals. Indeed, owner Safdie, author of two popular books, *Spa Food* and *New Spa Food*, believes in incorporating locally grown produce, fresh seafoods, and hearty game dishes in both the 850- or 1,200-calorie-a-day diet. Light and crusty Melba Meringues successfully complete any dinner, while the Honey Cinnamon Custard with Maple Syrup Sauce is so rich it is hard to believe it's low-cal.

Melba Meringues

The colors of this dessert—red, white, orange—
look sensational on a plate.

Preheat oven to 400°F
Cookie sheet sprayed with
   nonstick vegetable spray
Serves 4

2 cups fresh or frozen (thawed) raspberries honey to taste (optional)	Purée 1 cup berries. Strain and combine with other cup whole berries. Set aside.
2 egg whites	Beat until stiff in clean bowl.
1 tbsp. honey	Drizzle into whites and gently mix until combined.
2 fresh peaches, peeled, pitted, and halved	Place peaches cut side up on cookie sheet. Divide egg white mixture over top. Bake 4–5 minutes until golden. Divide raspberry mixture among 4 serving dishes. Gently place peach meringue on top.

Calories: 78

Protein: 2 g

Fat: 0.3 g

Cholesterol: 0 mg

Carbohydrates: 18 g

Sodium: 26 mg

Strawberry-Rhubarb Parfait

Strawberries and rhubarb have always been a great combination, especially when layered between honey orange yogurt.

6 individual dishes
Serves 6

**2 cups sliced rhubarb
(fresh or frozen—drained)
2 cups halved strawberries
¹/2 cup apple juice
2 tsp. grated orange rind
¹/2 cup fructose ***

Cook until soft, not mushy. Cool and strain. Set aside.

**2 cups low-fat yogurt
2 tbsp. orange juice
1 tbsp. honey
1 tsp. vanilla**

Combine until blended. In individual dishes, alternate layers of fruit mixture and yogurt mixture. Chill.

6 strawberries to garnish

*Fructose is a natural sweetener. For substitutes see page 6.

Calories:	144
Protein:	3 g
Fat:	0.9 g
Cholesterol:	2 mg
Carbohydrates:	32 g
Sodium:	30 mg

Poached Pear with Raspberry Purée

Raspberry and banana purée adds
sophistication to a simple dessert.

Serves 4

2 cups apple juice **1 cinnamon stick**	Place in pot over heat and bring to a boil.
2 medium pears	Peel and drop whole into boiling juice. Simmer until pears are done (fork-tender). Cool in juice. Meanwhile prepare purée.

Purée

2 cups raspberries **(fresh or frozen)** **¹/₂ ripe banana**	Purée, then strain through a sieve to remove seeds.
fructose * or sugar	Add a little if berries are not sweet enough.
	Pour some sauce on 4 individual dishes. Place ¹/₂ pear on each plate.
¹/₂ cup low-fat yogurt **(optional)**	Place in a squeeze bottle and squirt design around sauce.

*Fructose is a natural sweetener. For substitutes see page 6.

Calories: 182

Protein: 0.9 g

Fat: 0.5 g

Cholesterol: 0 mg

Carbohydrates: 45 g

Sodium: 7 mg

Oatmeal Raisin Cookies

After tasting these, children will never want chocolate chip cookies again.

Preheat oven to 375°F
Lightly grease a baking sheet
Makes approx. 18 cookies

2 oz. soft butter **6 tbsp. brown sugar**	Cream until smooth.
1 egg **1 tsp. vanilla extract**	Add and blend well.
¼ cup whole wheat flour **½ tsp. baking powder** **¼ cup wheat germ** **½ cup rolled oats** **½ cup raisins**	Add and stir in just until blended. Drop dough by teaspoonfuls on baking sheet, leaving 2″ between each cookie. Bake approx. 10–12 minutes and cool on racks.

Calories: 94

Protein: 2 g

Fat: 3 g

Cholesterol: 24 mg

Carbohydrates: 14 g

Sodium: 34 mg

Connecticut Baked Apples with Spa Cream

*Light spa cream turns simple baked apples
into a special dessert.*

Preheat oven to 350°F
Medium baking dish
Serves 4

2 medium red baking apples	Cut in half and core without cutting through to bottom. Place cut side up in baking dish.
apple juice	Pour just enough in baking dish to reach top of apples.
cinnamon **brown sugar**	Sprinkle a little over each apple half. Bake until slightly soft, not mushy, approx. 30 minutes. Cool to room temperature. Top with spa cream and garnish with cinnamon stick and mint leaf if desired.

Spa Cream

	Chill beaters and bowl in freezer.
½ cup skim milk	Chill in freezer until slushy.
½ tsp. vanilla **½ tsp. sugar**	Add to above. Beat in cold bowl until the consistency of whipped cream. Serve immediately with apples.

Calories: 99

Protein: 1 g

Fat: 0.3 g

Cholesterol: 0.5 mg

Carbohydrates: 24 g

Sodium: 19 mg

Honey Cinnamon Custard with Maple Syrup Sauce

Rich maple syrup sauce completes this light cinnamon custard.

Preheat oven to 300°F
Lightly grease a 1 qt. soufflé dish
Serves 8

4 eggs **1 egg white** **¼ tsp. ground cinnamon** **¼ tsp. ground nutmeg** **⅓ cup honey** **2½ cups whole milk**	Combine well until all ingredients are blended. Pour into dish and place in a larger pan filled with hot water (bain-marie). Bake until custard is set, approx. 80 minutes. Let cool. Chill until cold. Serve with sauce.

Maple Syrup Sauce

1 egg yolk	Whisk until thick and lemon colored. Set aside.
¼ cup maple syrup	Bring to a boil. Pour over egg yolk. Whisk constantly. Chill.
4 drops vanilla extract **1¾ cups cold skim milk**	In bowl, whip until foamy and thick. Fold into cold maple syrup mixture. Serve immediately with chilled custard.

Calories:	187
Protein:	9 g
Fat:	6 g
Cholesterol:	195 mg
Carbohydrates:	23 g
Sodium:	127 mg

Pineapple Lime Sorbet

A combination of pineapple and lime or lemon juice is refreshing after or in between a meal.

Serves 4

1¼ cups pineapple purée
¾ cup lime or lemon juice
2 tsp. grated lime or lemon rind
¼ cup water
sweetener to taste if needed *

Fresh lime or lemon slices to garnish

Combine and freeze in ice-cream maker or pour into pan and freeze until nearly solid. Chop into smaller pieces, purée, and refreeze. Serve in 4 individual dessert dishes.

*See sweeteners, page 6.

Calories:	56
Protein:	0.5 g
Fat:	0.2 g
Cholesterol:	0 mg
Carbohydrates:	15 g
Sodium:	10 mg

Cal-a-Vie, one of the newest entries on the spa scene, may also be one of the most exclusive. In a wooded valley tucked amidst the rolling hills of North San Diego County, 125 acres are devoted to peace and tranquility. Having a maximum of only twenty-four guests per week assures each one of them highly personalized attention.

Founder William Power made his mark in the Southern California health care industry. With wife, Marlene, and daughter, Susan, he opened Cal-a-Vie in 1986 because he saw stress as the number one health problem in America and wanted to find a solution.

Each guest cottage is a mélange of English country, French provincial, and Mediterranean architectural influences. Terra cotta roofs, wide doors, hand-carved furniture, and window boxes brimming with flowers are the essence of these country dwellings. The pastoral grounds are ablaze with orange nasturtiums, blue agapanthus, and a spectrum of daylilies with a serene stream gurgling through the center.

At Cal-a-Vie all guests are assessed by computer analysis for their general level of fitness. The program has been developed to encourage a balanced lifestyle for the individual. Fitness activities range from body alignment, posture, and movement classes to aerobics and body contouring. Also offered are swimming, yoga, t'ai chi, tennis, and golf.

The full range of massage and beauty treatments includes hydrotherapy, an underwater lymphatic massage; a cycle of green coating called body wrapping, leaving the skin rose-petal soft; and Aromatherapy, a rub down with oils to alleviate specific problems—lavender or orange for calming tension, apricot for insomnia, and juniper for water retention.

Cal-a-Vie cuisine, characterized by low-calorie, gourmet meals, is highlighted by herbs and vegetables from Cal-a-Vie's garden. Meals are artfully presented to slim, balance, and revitalize your body while meeting unique nutritional needs. The grand finale capping a savory meal is the Cal-a-Vie dessert experience—simple, low-calorie, yet exquisite both in taste and presentation.

Mocha Parfait

This resembles a light coffee mousse.

6 individual serving dishes
  or champagne glasses
Serves 6

⅓ cup double strength coffee (chilled)
⅙ cup nonfat powdered milk
1 tbsp. Kahlua or other chocolate liqueur
2½ cups small ice cubes or crushed ice
3 tbsp. honey

Blend in food processor until thickened like whipped cream. Spoon into serving dishes.

¼ cup toasted sliced almonds—sprinkle over top

Serve immediately or chill in freezer for only a short time (15 minutes) before serving. (Decorate with a coffee bean if desired.)

Do not allow to stay in freezer too long or consistency will not be properly maintained.

Calories: 49

Protein: 2 g

Fat: 3 g

Cholesterol: 0.3 mg

Carbohydrates: 3 g

Sodium: 12 mg

Chocolate Swirl Pie

This beautiful chocolate pie was featured in the May 1990 issue of Chocolatier *magazine.*

9″ pie pan sprayed with
   nonstick vegetable spray
Serves 12

Crust

1 1/2 cups graham cracker crumbs (preferably whole wheat)
1 tbsp. brown sugar
1/2 tsp. cinnamon
3 tbsp. butter cut into cubes
1 large egg white

Combine in food processor and pat onto sides and bottom of pie pan.

Filling

3 oz. semi-sweet chocolate

Melt and set aside.

12 oz. fresh tofu (room temperature)
1/2 cup plain low-fat yogurt (room temperature)
1/4 cup honey
2 large eggs
2 tsp. vanilla extract
1/4 tsp. salt

In food processor, combine until well mixed. Pour into pie pan. Pour melted chocolate into a pastry bag fitted with a narrow tip, or into a squeezable plastic bottle. Draw lines across pie at 1″ intervals. With a toothpick or bamboo skewer, pull chocolate outward to create swirl-like effect as in photo. Bake for approx. 30 minutes, or until pie is set (the center will shake a little). Cool and refrigerate for 2 hours.

Calories:	187
Protein:	5 g
Fat:	8 g
Cholesterol:	43 mg
Carbohydrates:	21 g
Sodium:	182 mg

Orange Kiwi Sorbet

*The combination of oranges and kiwis
is light and refreshing.*

Serves 4

4 medium juicy oranges

Cut off top $\frac{1}{3}$ of oranges and cut a thin slice off the bottom to keep oranges standing. Make orange juice from the oranges and place empty orange shells in the freezer, along with tops.

2 kiwis, peeled and quartered
1 tsp. fructose *
$\frac{1}{2}$ tbsp. orange liqueur (optional)

Purée orange juice, kiwis, fructose, and liqueur. Pour into ice-cream maker and freeze or pour into loaf pan. Freeze until nearly solid, then purée and scoop into frozen orange shells. Replace tops and decorate with berries.

Fresh berries for garnish

*Fructose is a natural sweetener.
For substitutes see page 6.

Calories:	108
Protein:	2 g
Fat:	0.5 g
Cholesterol:	0 mg
Carbohydrates:	26 g
Sodium:	5 mg

Butternut Squash Flan

Creamy butternut squash tastes like a pumpkin tart.

Preheat oven to 350°F
6 individual custard cups or
  6 cup baking dish
Serves 6

Fresh or prepackaged butternut squash equaling 1 lb. of pulp	If squash is prepacked, cook until soft. If squash is fresh, bake at 350°F for approx. 1–1½ hours. Peel off skin, deseed, and purée pulp.
½ tsp. cinnamon ***¼ tsp. ground cloves*** ***⅛ tsp. grated nutmeg*** ***½ tsp. vanilla extract*** ***4 tbsp. honey***	Add and purée until smooth.
1¼ cups low-fat milk	Scald milk.
1 egg ***1 egg white***	Place eggs in separate bowl and whip in scalded milk. Strain into puréed squash mixture and mix well.
	Pour into individual dishes or one larger dish. Bake in a water bath for approx. 45 minutes for smaller dishes and one hour for larger dish, or until knife comes out clean.

Calories: 114

Protein: 4 g

Fat: 3 g

Cholesterol: 54 mg

Carbohydrates: 20 g

Sodium: 48 mg

Fruit Mosaic with Sabayon Sauce

This creamy sauce with a beautiful array of fruits actually resembles a mosaic.

5 individual ovenproof dessert dishes
Serves 5

Sabayon

3 egg yolks
¹/₂ cup white wine
2 tbsp. sweet wine
1 tbsp. orange liqueur
1 tsp. grated lemon peel

In double boiler, over medium heat, whisk until smooth and thick, approx. 3 minutes. Do not boil, or eggs will curdle. Remove from heat.

Sweetener to equal 2 tsp. sugar (optional) *

If more sweetness is desired, add and continue whisking until smooth. Cool. Spread sabayon over bottom of 5 dessert dishes.

Fruit**

2 kiwis, peeled and sliced
1 cup fresh raspberries
2 oranges cut in segments
5 strawberries

Arrange in a colorful pattern over sabayon.

4 tbsp. ground almonds

Sprinkle over fruit. Bake under broiler just until browned (2–3 minutes).

*For sweeteners, see page 6.
**Any fresh fruit desired will do.

Calories:	157
Protein:	4 g
Fat:	7 g
Cholesterol:	163 mg
Carbohydrates:	20 g
Sodium:	9 mg

Vanilla Almond Snaps
Sonoma Mission Inn and Spa,
California

Chocolate Seashells
The Golden Door,
California

Tulip Cookies with
Fruit Sorbet
Doral Saturnia,
Florida

Cinnamon Date
Coffee Cake
King Ranch,
Toronto

Frozen Lemon Roulade
Rancho La Puerta,
Mexico

Apple Strudel
The Heartland,
Illinois

Doral
SATURNIA

There are many international spas in the United States, but Doral Saturnia may be the most beautiful. It is here that American fitness techniques combine with old-world European soothing treatments to renew both body and soul in a breathtaking environment.

At Doral Saturnia, the emphasis is on balancing fitness, nutrition, stress management, and total image. Guests at this lavish resort/spa are challenged and pampered, guided and given freedom to choose.

The Spa Centre and luxury Spa Villa hotel expand over 148,000 square feet. International architects and interior designers have restored the grandeur and history of Tuscany within the tropical wonder and beauty of Florida. Several suites are inspired by Italian cities, transporting guests back to the Etruscan period by employing warm terra cotta, black, and eggshell, and stenciled *trompe l'oeil* frescoes. The "Sardinia" suites utilize seaside symbols for bright, clean, yet sophisticated interiors. Throughout the Spa Centre and Villa are remarkable works of art: a contemporary tapestry by renowned weaver Sylvia Heyden; an exquisite tie-dye hanging of a wooded scene; witty modern paintings; and striking life-size mural reproductions of Botticelli's most exquisite Renaissance masterpieces.

Fitness programs include exercise on land and in water, indoor and outdoor pools, a banked track with its own sound system, an exercise trail set in the lush tropical landscape, and the lighter, quieter, easier to use David high-tech resistance fitness equipment. Guests enjoy tennis, riding, golf, and unusual sports like croquet and *bocce* (lawn bowling).

Stress is relieved with a multitude of water and body therapies, including mineral and plankton baths to rejuvenate. Guided imagery, yoga, and biofeedback create a new and positive self inside that reflects outside.

Gourmet spa cuisine, not surprisingly, utilizes the best of Italian cooking, reducing fat and calories but leaving taste intact. Refreshing Tulip Cookies with Fruit Sorbet, a fitting finish to any meal, and Cinnamon Carrot Cake delight even the most jaded palate.

Blueberry Apple Crisp

This outstanding crisp is better than any other I have ever tasted and has one quarter the calories!

Preheat oven to 350°F
9″ baking pan
Serves 10

½ *pint blueberries*
3 *medium apples, cored and sliced*
1 *tbsp. lemon juice*
¼ *cup apple juice*
1 *tsp. cinnamon*
2 *tbsp. sugar*

Mix and place in bottom of pan.

⅛ *cup apple juice*
1 *cup rolled oats*
⅓ *cup whole wheat flour*
¼ *cup brown sugar*
2 *tbsp. butter*
½ *tsp. cinnamon*

Mix together, then sprinkle over blueberry apple mixture. Bake for 30 minutes or until golden brown.

Calories:	115
Protein:	1 g
Fat:	2 g
Cholesterol:	5 mg
Carbohydrates:	23 g
Sodium:	20 mg

Orange Coffee Cake

A light yet rich-tasting coffee cake.

Preheat oven to 350°F
Use a Bundt pan lightly sprayed with
   nonstick vegetable spray
Serves 10–12

4 tbsp. butter **1 cup sugar**	Cream together.
3 medium eggs	Add one at a time and beat after each addition. Set aside.
1 cup whole wheat flour **1 cup white flour** **2 tsp. baking soda**	Combine in bowl. Set aside.
2 cups orange juice **2 tsp. orange zest**	Boil and then chill, just until cool to touch.
	Add flour and juice mixture to above butter mixture in thirds, beating after each addition, just until well combined. Pour into pan and bake for 35–40 minutes or until tester comes out clean. Cool on rack and invert.
Powdered sugar and **fresh sliced strawberries** **for garnish**	

Calories: 136

Protein: 3 g

Fat: 3 g

Cholesterol: 51 mg

Carbohydrates: 24 g

Sodium: 225 mg

Tulip Cookies with Fruit Sorbet

*Refreshing fruit sorbets are delightful
with this light crispy cookie.*

Preheat oven to 350°F
2 cookie sheets sprayed with
  nonstick vegetable spray
Serves approx. 20

6 tbsp. sugar
⅛ tsp. cinnamon
⅛ tsp. salt
5 tbsp. whole wheat flour
5 tbsp. white flour
1 egg
¾ cup buttermilk

Mix all ingredients in bowl and let sit for 20 minutes. Place 1 tbsp. of cookie batter on one half of cookie sheet. Spread with the back of a spoon to form thin circular shape approx. 5″ in diameter. Repeat with another tbsp. on other side of cookie sheet. Repeat with second sheet and bake for approx. 9–11 minutes or until lightly brown. Remove with spatula quickly and place over bottom of (inverted) small cup or glass. Press firmly to shape into tulip cups. Repeat until all batter is used. (Lightly respray cookie sheets before each use.) Serve with 3 small scoops of sorbet or ice milk.

**Fruit sorbet or ice milk of
choice (see index)**

Calories:	60
Protein:	2 g
Fat:	0.4 g
Cholesterol:	12 mg
Carbohydrates:	13 g
Sodium:	37 mg

In the midst of flat Illinois farm country, surrounded by miles of cornfields, lies a thirty-acre wooded estate. Resting beside Kam Lake, The Heartland is a peaceful, deliciously isolated spa dedicated to stress management.

Twenty-eight guests with hectic lifestyles are drawn each week to this spa eighty miles south of Chicago. Furnished in middle-American pine, the thirteen private guest rooms are familiarly cozy, comfortable, and quaint. This spa provides most personal amenities, from shampoo to a complete fitness wardrobe, even an evening leisure-wear outfit plus wool hat and gloves, socks, slippers, and a thick terry-cloth bathrobe. The Mansion, or main building, has a library, parlor, dining room, and living room where informal socializing takes place. In The Barn, a multilevel fitness center, exercise classes are always in process, from easy bodywork aerobics to one-and-a-half-hour superclasses of stretching, aerobic workout, and calisthenics. The focus at The Heartland ranges from general fitness and weight loss to a special emphasis on cardiovascular conditioning and learning how to manage stress. This spa prides itself on utilizing the most current, accurate scientific information available regarding fitness and diet, encouraging high-powered people to learn the difference between harmful stress and stress that enhances life. High-tech pneumatic resistance equipment, gravity-inversion equipment, and free weights are available, as well as outdoor jogging, Parcours (an obstacle course to improve flexibility, balance, agility, and strength), tennis, cross-country skiing, swimming, and cycling around the lake. After exercise, relaxing in a rock sauna, steam room, or whirlpool, or indulging in a massage (four types are available—sports, relaxation, foot, and injury) will completely relax both mind and body. Guests enjoy facials, manicures, cosmetic consultation, and a unique deep pore cleansing and conditioning for the back.

The menu is low-fat, low-calorie, and vegetarian, with such unusual entrees as pizza and tostadas. Desserts, too, are special. For example, Berry Yogurt Parfait and Blueberry Nut Cake are guaranteed to reduce stress.

Maple Flan with Walnuts

*With or without the cinnamon cream,
this maple dessert is heavenly.*

Preheat oven to 325°F
1 quart baking dish
Serves 6

1 egg *** 2 egg whites*** ***2¹/₂ tbsp. maple syrup*** ***1 tsp. vanilla extract*** ***1 tsp. maple extract*** ***(more if desired for taste)***	Blend until smooth.
1¹/₂ cups 2% milk	Add to above slowly, whisking constantly. Pour into dish and bake in water bath (bain-marie) approx. 60 minutes or until mixture looks set. Serve with cinnamon cream if desired (page 128).
Sprinkle lighly with chopped nuts	

Calories:	87
Protein:	4 g
Fat:	3 g
Cholesterol:	54 mg
Carbohydrates:	10 g
Sodium:	65 mg

Blueberry Nut Cake

A nice change from coffee cake.
Great as a morning bread or evening dessert.

Preheat oven to 350°F
9″ springform pan or baking dish
   sprayed with nonstick vegetable spray
30 small squares

½ cup soft butter *½ cup honey*	Cream until smooth.
1¼ cups 2% milk *3 eggs*	Add to above and mix until well combined. Mixture will curdle.
2¼ cups whole wheat flour *1 tbsp. baking powder* *1 tsp. nutmeg* *2 tsp. cinnamon*	Sift and add to above creamed mixture until just combined.
¾ cup blueberries *½ cup walnuts*	Add to above until all is incorporated. Do not overmix. Pour into pan and bake for approx. 25–30 minutes or until tester comes out clean.

Calories: 100

Protein: 2 g

Fat: 5 g

Cholesterol: 39 mg

Carbohydrates: 11 g

Sodium: 48 mg

Frozen Jamoca Mousse

For all coffee lovers.
Tastes like a rich ice cream.

Serves approx. 12

**7¹/₂ oz. ricotta cheese
(low-fat)
2 cups yogurt (low-fat)
1¹/₄ tbsp. cocoa powder
³/₄ tbsp. instant coffee
¹/₂ cup fructose *
1 tsp. vanilla**

Blend in food processor until smooth. Place mixture in ice-cream maker until frozen. If ice-cream maker is not available, place mixture in bowl and freeze until almost solid. Process in food processor until creamy. Refreeze.

*Fructose is a natural sweetener. For substitutes see page 6.

Calories:	77
Protein:	3 g
Fat:	2 g
Cholesterol:	7 mg
Carbohydrates:	11 g
Sodium:	39 mg

Date Nut Bar

This multipurpose treat can be enjoyed as a nutritious snack, dessert, or even breakfast accompaniment.

8″ pan
Serves 16

1 1/3 cups chopped pitted dates
1/4 cup walnut pieces
1/4 cup almonds

Place in a food processor and blend until mixture begins to come together. Set aside.

1/2 cup granola

Place 1/4 cup granola into pan and press date mixture firmly over top. Top with remaining granola. Chill and cut into squares.

Calories: 83

Protein: 1 g

Fat: 3 g

Cholesterol: 0 mg

Carbohydrates: 13 g

Sodium: 1 mg

Frozen Orange Cream

*This light fruit sorbet is excellent after a meal
or in between to clear the palate.*

Serves 4

⅔ cup skim milk
1⅓ cups orange juice
peel of 1 orange grated
finely

Place in blender or food processor and mix. Place in ice-cream machine and freeze, or alternatively place in bowl and freeze until nearly solid. Process until creamy and refreeze.

Calories:	49
Protein:	2 g
Fat:	0.1 g
Cholesterol:	0.7 mg
Carbohydrates:	10 g
Sodium:	22 mg

Strawberry or Peach Crêpes

Crêpes have made a real comeback,
since they are a light finish to any meal
and shells can be prepared in advance and frozen.

Serves 8

Crêpes (page 31)

Filling

3 cups strawberries or peaches　　Cut into small pieces.

1 cup ricotta cheese
2 tbsp. honey
2 tsp. vanilla

Blend until smooth in food processsor. Add cut fruit, mix, and divide among 8 crêpes. Roll crêpes and serve.

Calories:	115
Protein:	6 g
Fat:	3 g
Cholesterol:	30 mg
Carbohydrates:	15 g
Sodium:	70 mg

Pumpkin Flan

A light and spicy pumpkin-lovers' fantasy.

Preheat oven to 325°F
6 individual custard cups or
   1 qt. custard bowl
Serves 6

1 cup 2% milk

Bring to near boil over low heat.

2 egg whites
1 egg
½ tsp. almond extract
⅛ tsp. ground cloves
¼ tsp. cinnamon
2½ tbsp. fructose *
½ tsp. vanilla
¾ cup pumpkin

In bowl mix all other ingredients until smooth. Whisk hot milk into this mixture. Pour into individual custard cups or 1 quart custard bowl. Bake in water bath (bain-marie) until custard is set, approx. 20 minutes for small cups, or 40 minutes for larger bowl.

Serve with cinnamon cream.

Cinnamon Cream

1 cup low-fat ricotta cheese
1½ tbsp. honey or
maple syrup
¾ tsp. ground cinnamon

Combine in food processor until smooth.

*Fructose is a natural sweetener. For substitutes see page 6.

Calories:	111
Protein:	6 g
Fat:	3 g
Cholesterol:	60 mg
Carbohydrates:	13 g
Sodium:	75 mg

Applesauce Carrot Cake

The applesauce makes this style of carrot cake moist and light.

Preheat oven to 350°F
Bundt pan sprayed with
   nonstick vegetable spray
Makes 32 small pieces

1 cup unsweetened applesauce *3 eggs* *5 tbsp. corn oil* *2 tsp. baking powder* *1 tsp. baking soda* *¼ tsp. salt* *¾ cup honey* *1¼ tbsp. ground cinnamon* *¼ tsp. allspice* *½ tsp. nutmeg* *2⅓ cups whole wheat flour*	Combine in large bowl until well blended.
2 cups grated carrots	Add until just blended. Pour into pan and bake for approx. 35 minutes or until tester comes out clean. Cool on rack. Refrigerate. (If desired, frost with lemon cream frosting, page 132.)

Calories: 75

Protein: 2 g

Fat: 2 g

Cholesterol: 28 mg

Carbohydrates: 11 g

Sodium: 90 mg

Apple Strudel with Cinnamon Sauce

This strudel is great when served warm,
with or without the cinnamon sauce.

Preheat oven to 400°F
1 baking sheet
Serves 8

1¼ lbs. apples (approx. 4 apples)	Peel, core, and slice.
½ tsp. cinnamon *¼ tsp. nutmeg* *¼ cup raisins (optional)* *1 tbsp. fructose* *	Mix with apples.
4 phyllo sheets	Place sheets on top of each other and spread apple mixture over top sheet. If desired, spray each sheet with a little nonstick vegetable spray. Roll up carefully. Bake approx. 25–30 minutes or until lightly browned. Serve with cinnamon sauce.

Cinnamon Sauce

1 cup apple cider *2 tsp. arrowroot or cornstarch dissolved in* *1 tbsp. water*	Combine in small saucepan. Whisk constantly until mixture comes to a boil and has thickened. Serve warm.

*Fructose is a natural sweetener. For substitutes see page 6.

Calories: 168

Protein: 2 g

Fat: 2 g

Cholesterol: 0 mg

Carbohydrates: 36 g

Sodium: 97 mg

Peanut Butter Granola Rolls

Both children and adults will devour these scrumptious peanut butter balls.

Makes approx. 40 balls

¼ *cup raisins*
¾ *cup peanut butter*
¼ *cup apple butter* *

Process until raisins are finely chopped.

1½ *cups granola*
¼ *cup water*

Alternately add and process until mixture comes together.

2 *tbsp. wheat germ*

Roll above mixture into 1 tbsp. balls, then roll in wheat germ.

* Available in peanut butter section of stores or in health food stores. Substitute peanut butter if unable to find.

Calories:	52
Protein:	2 g
Fat:	3 g
Cholesterol:	0 mg
Carbohydrates:	4 g
Sodium:	20 mg

Banana Cake with Lemon Cream Frosting

A moist and luscious banana cake, with or without the frosting.
But try this unusual frosting—it is fabulous.

Preheat oven to 350°F
9″x13″ baking pan sprayed with
   nonstick vegetable spray
25 small squares

¼ cup oil (preferably walnut oil) *½ cup honey* *3 medium bananas* *½ cup buttermilk*	Combine in food processor until smooth.
1¾ cups whole wheat flour *2 tsp. baking powder* *¾ tsp. baking soda*	Stir into above until just mixed.
4 egg whites	Beat in clean bowl until stiff, then fold into above mixture. Pour into pan and bake for 20–30 minutes or until tester comes out clean. When cool, frost with icing.

Lemon Cream Frosting

8 oz. low-fat ricotta cheese *1 tbsp. lemon juice* *1½ tbsp. honey* *½ tbsp. arrowroot or cornstarch* *zest from one lemon*	Combine in food processor and process until smooth. Place in a saucepan and heat until nearly boiling. Stir constantly to prevent scorching. Chill. Frost top of cake.
4 tbsp. chopped walnuts	Sprinkle with nuts.

Calories: 85

Protein: 2 g

Fat: 2 g

Cholesterol: 2 mg

Carbohydrates: 14 g

Sodium: 64 mg

Angel Food Cake with Puréed Pears

A light and airy cake, perfect for dessert or tea time.
The pear sauce adds an unusual taste to angel food cake.

Preheat oven to 300°F
10″ Bundt or tube pan ungreased
24 slices

12 large egg whites **1 tsp. cream of tartar** **¼ tsp. salt**	Beat to soft peaks.
1 cup fructose *	Fold in 2 tbsp. at a time until all incorporated.
1¼ cups sifted pastry flour **1½ tsp. vanilla extract** **¾ tsp. almond extract** **¾ tsp. lemon extract**	Fold in gently to above mixture, just until all is blended. Do not overfold. Bake for approx. 50–60 minutes, or until tester comes out dry. Invert and cool for one hour. Remove with the help of a knife around the sides of the pan.

Puréed Pears

18 oz. pears, peeled and sliced (approx. 4 pears)	Set aside.
2 fruit-flavored tea bags **2 cups water** **1 tbsp. fructose *** **1 tsp. almond extract**	Bring to a boil and simmer for 5 minutes. Remove tea bags. Add pears and simmer for 5 minutes. (Pears should still be firm.) Remove pears from liquid and cool. Save poaching liquid. Purée pears into a sauce. To serve, place a piece of cake on a plate, pour a little poaching liquid and pear sauce over top.

*Fructose is a natural sweetener.
For substitutes see page 6.

Calories: 83

Protein: 2 g

Fat: 0 g

Cholesterol: 0 mg

Carbohydrates: 18 g

Sodium: 54 mg

133

The doors have recently opened at Canada's first international health spa and
fitness resort. Already this spa is deluged with rave reviews.

One of the reasons the Koffler family opened the 177-acre spa/resort
in historic King Township, just north of their home in Toronto, was to
realize their ambition of catering to "today's goal-oriented, active people,
professionals and executives recharging their batteries."

The seasonal changes of lush meadows, wooded hills, and verdant
countryside play an integral role in spa life here. The clubhouse, 120 guest
residences, and spa, designed by world-renowned architect Arthur
Erickson, are interconnected for easy access. Buildings relate harmoniously
to the landscape, and vaulted glass windows invite the great outdoors inside.
Relaxed elegance produced by this contemporary and natural ambience,
with fieldstone fireplaces, cedar beams, slate floors, and all Canadian art,
makes King Ranch a refuge for all guests seeking health, well-being, and
renewal. Comprehensive programs include a full range of over thirty fitness
classes, aerobic gyms, indoor-outdoor pools, weight rooms, racquet courts,
and the *pièce de résistance*—a spectacular elevated indoor/outdoor track
that allows joggers to tune into nature while burning calories. Changing
seasons offer hiking, horseback riding, cross-country skiing, skating, and
snowshoeing. Beauty and relaxation treatments run the gamut: Swedish
massage, shiatsu, aromatherapy, sports massage, herbal wraps, cellular
rejuvenation, hydrotherapy, hair and scalp treatments, skin analysis, beauty
treatments, and more. For evening entertainment, King Ranch has a fully
equipped private movie theater, with Dolby sound. At the spa's International
Waters Bar, guests choose from a wide range of imported spring and mineral waters. A trip into the world-class city of Toronto, only twenty-five miles
away, with its multitude of shopping and cultural opportunities, is an option.

Enlightened spa cuisine creates healthy and appealing meals. For
dinner parties or even just family suppers, try these exciting desserts: Chocolate Brownies, Cinnamon Date Coffee Cake, or Banana Crêpes with
Orange Sauce.

Chocolate Brownies

Rich, torte-like brownies.

Preheat oven to 350°F
8″ baking dish sprayed with
   nonstick vegetable spray
Makes 16 squares

6 oz. semi-sweet chocolate
¹/₂ cup hot water

Melt and stir until smooth.

²/₃ cup sugar
1 tsp. vanilla extract
4 egg whites
²/₃ cup flour
1 tsp. baking powder
¹/₈ tsp. salt

Add and mix until combined.
Pour into pan and bake
approx. 25–30 minutes, just
until center is slightly loose.
Cool. Sprinkle with powdered
sugar, or place yogurt in squeeze
bottle and squeeze design over
brownies (see page 11).

Calories:	130
Protein:	3 g
Fat:	5 g
Cholesterol:	20 mg
Carbohydrates:	40 g
Sodium:	62 mg

Cinnamon Date Coffee Cake

A light cinnamon cake with small bitefuls of dates.

Preheat oven to 350°F
9″ Bundt pan sprayed with
nonstick vegetable spray
Makes 16 slices

3 tbsp. soft butter **¾ cup sugar** **1 egg** **2 egg whites**	Cream together until smooth.
1⅓ cup low-fat yogurt **1 tsp. vanilla** **1 tsp. cinnamon** **⅛ tsp. nutmeg** **3 tbsp. lemon juice**	Add to above and mix until combined.
2 cups flour **1 tsp. baking powder** **1 tsp. baking soda**	Sift, and mix with above just until combined.
4 tbsp. brown sugar **⅔ cup chopped dates**	Mix in small bowl. Pour half of the above cake batter into pan and sprinkle half of date mixture over top. Pour in remaining batter and sprinkle remaining date mixture on top. Bake for approx. 40 minutes, or until tester comes out clean. Cool. Sprinkle with powdered sugar.

Calories: 163

Protein: 3.6 g

Fat: 1.9 g

Cholesterol: 33.6 mg

Carbohydrates: 24 g

Sodium: 69 mg

Banana Crêpes with Orange Sauce

Bananas and orange juice together with the spice cardamom are a great combination.

6 individual plates
Serves 6

Crêpes (page 31)	
⅓ tsp. cardamom	Add to crêpe recipe. When completed, set crêpes in a warm place, covered with a towel.
2½ cups orange juice or juice of approx. 8 oranges	Over medium heat, reduce the orange juice to one half its original volume. Remove from heat and set aside.
2 large bananas	Cut each into approx. 9 pieces.
1 tbsp. butter	Sauté bananas in butter over high heat until hot and golden brown. Divide orange juice among 6 plates.
1 orange, peeled and broken into wedges	Garnish plates with orange sections. Divide the hot banana pieces among 6 crêpes, roll, and place over juice on plate.

Calories: 211

Protein: 4 g

Fat: 3 g

Cholesterol: 26 mg

Carbohydrates: 44 g

Sodium: 52 mg

One of North America's unique spas lies forty miles southeast of San Diego. Located on 150 acres in Baja California, just across the Mexican border, Rancho La Puerta rates as perhaps the most easygoing resort spa-goers are likely to find.

The fifty-year-old establishment was the first residential spa in this continent. What has become the norm at fitness retreats—devotion to health dawn to dusk—originated here where, at inception, the idea was considered avant garde.

Baja is desert country, a gentle and dry climate, but owners Edmond and Deborah Szekely have made the parched earth bloom while retaining the flavor of old Mexico. Wild lilacs, irises, and poppies, hummingbirds in the bougainvillea, sunflowers and sage, vineyards, hawks, quail, coyotes—nature is here at its most unspoiled.

Guests are housed in private one-of-a-kind haciendas built of local brick and quarried stone, many with fireplaces. Decor is strictly Mexican—handwoven cloth in the brightest reds, yellows, and blues in the world. Mount Cuchuma's hilly terrain, at 1,800 feet, offers plenty of hiking trails. The ratio of guests (150 maximum) to staff is an astonishing one-to-one. Because the Szekelys believe exercise needs of men and women differ, they provide separate facilities for fitness and relaxation, which includes nude sunbathing. But aerobic and other workout classes are coed, as well as the six lighted tennis courts, four swimming pools, and an abundance of Mexican hammocks for quiet naps. Swedish massage, Kneipp herbal wraps, facials, and scalp treatments are offered both sexes.

Rancho La Puerta might be the birthplace of spa cuisine. A lacto-ovo modified vegetarian diet is employed. One thousand calories a day of all-natural food—low in sodium, cholesterol, and refined sugar, high in fiber and complex carbohydrates, grown without toxic pesticides and fertilizers—could accurately be termed "honest food." Fruits from the garden are utilized for desserts like Frozen Lemon Roulade, Strawberry Shortcake, and a superb Orange Yogurt Cream that tastes fresher than fresh.

Frozen Lemon Roulade

This lemony roll cake is wonderfully refreshing.
Puréed strawberries add a beautiful color contrast.

Preheat oven to 375°F
9″x13″ jelly roll pan sprayed with
   nonstick vegetable spray and lined with
   parchment paper
Makes 20 slices

5 eggs **½ cup fructose ***	Beat for approx. 5 minutes until thick and creamy.
1¼ tsp. nutmeg **1 tsp. vanilla** **1 tsp. lemon zest**	Add to above and combine.
¾ cup flour	Fold into above just until combined. Pour into pan and bake approx. 12–15 minutes until puffy and lightly browned. Invert onto another sheet of parchment paper and carefully peel away cooked paper. Place tea towel over top and set aside.

Lemon Ice Milk

1½–2 pints vanilla ice milk **or frozen yogurt softened** **(see page 95)** **½ cup lemon juice** **2 tbsp. lemon zest** **1 tsp. lemon extract** **(optional)**	Beat well until all combined. Spread ice milk evenly over top of genoise. Roll up and wrap in plastic wrap and freeze until ready to serve.
½ cup strawberry purée or **1 cup sliced strawberries**	Slice cake thinly and serve with strawberries. Sprinkle powdered sugar lightly over cake if desired.

Calories: 135

Protein: 3 g

Fat: 4 g

Cholesterol: 87 mg

Carbohydrates: 20 g

Sodium: 43 mg

*Fructose is a natural sweetener.
For substitutes see page 6.

Strawberry Shortcake

*Miniature shortcakes can be served with pastry cream,
orange yogurt cream, or even just sliced strawberries.
Any combination is great.*

Preheat oven to 350°F
6 cup muffin tin lightly sprayed
   with nonstick vegetable spray
Serves 6

2 eggs **½ cup fructose *** **or ¾ cup sugar**	Beat for at least 5 minutes until thick and creamy.
1 pinch nutmeg **¼ tsp. vanilla** **⅛ tsp. ground cardamom (optional)**	Add and beat into above.
⅓ cup flour	Fold into above. Pour into muffin tin and bake approx. 10–12 minutes, until lightly browned and no longer wet. Remove from tins and cool completely.

Assembly

1 cup orange yogurt cream (page 142) or **1 cup pastry cream (page 21)** **1 cup sliced strawberries or** **½ cup puréed strawberries**	Split shortcakes in half and fill each with a small amount of either orange yogurt cream or pastry cream. Serve with sliced or puréed strawberries.

*Fructose is a natural sweetener.
For substitutes see page 6.

Calories: 149

Protein: 4 g

Fat: 2 g

Cholesterol: 80 mg

Carbohydrates: 26 g

Sodium: 39 mg

Orange Yogurt Cream*

This needs to be made in advance but will keep for several days in the refrigerator and is well worth having on hand.

Serves 8

2 cups plain yogurt

Pour into metal strainer lined with cheesecloth or J cloth. Place bowl underneath to catch drippings. Refrigerate at least 12 hours. Remove cloth and combine with following ingredients.

¹/₂ tbsp. orange juice concentrate
¹/₂ tbsp. Grand Marnier
¹/₂ tbsp. fructose ** or**
³/₄ tbsp. sugar
¹/₂ tbsp. grated orange peel

Mix, then add to above.

*Pastry cream can be substituted for yogurt cream in recipes (see page 21).
**Fructose is a natural sweetener. For substitutes see page 6.

Calories: 23

Protein: 1 g

Fat: 0.4 g

Cholesterol: 2 mg

Carbohydrates: 2.7 g

Sodium: 21 mg

Strawberries Grand Marnier

*Simple strawberries can be turned into
a sophisticated dessert with a touch
of liqueur and pastry cream.*

Individual champagne glasses
Serves 4

1 cup orange juice *2 tsp. fructose* or* *3 tsp. sugar* *2 tsp. Grand Marnier*	Combine.
2 cups sliced strawberries	Add to above and let marinate in refrigerator for 30 minutes.
1 cup orange yogurt cream (page 142) *or pastry cream (page 21)* *strawberries and/or orange zest as garnish*	Divide above strawberry mixture into individual glasses. Place some orange yogurt cream or pastry cream over strawberries.

*Fructose is a natural sweetener.
For substitutes see page 6.

Calories:	90
Protein:	2 g
Fat:	0.8 g
Cholesterol:	2 mg
Carbohydrates:	18 g
Sodium:	23 mg

Fruit Coulis (Purée)

A simple purée that goes with many different desserts.
Almost any fruit can be substituted.

Makes 1 cup

8 oz. weighed (2 cups measured) fresh or frozen (thawed) strawberries, raspberries, or blueberries

Purée. Sieve fruit to remove seeds.

Calories: 15

Protein: 0.2 g

Fat: 0.1 g

Cholesterol: 0 mg

Carbohydrates: 2 g

Sodium: 0.3 mg

In the elite world of spas, one establishment stands a notch above the rest. Even spa owners in need of rejuvenation gravitate to Jimmy Lesage's New Life Spa.

More than a decade ago, dynamic founder Jimmy Lesage started a trend. He put into practice a novel approach to health—wellness as an ongoing process. Lesage's broad-based credentials—history degree, training in haute cuisine, hotel management, contributions to the New England Cardiovascular Health Institute on prevention of heart and degenerative diseases, and an extensive study of yoga at the famous Sivanada Yoga Retreat—mean that guests at Lesage's New Life Spa enjoy a comprehensive yet realistic approach to health. Programs, comfortably limited to forty participants, are geared to a variety of ages and physical conditions.

At the base of Vermont's Stratton Mountains, guests lodge in two-story Austrian-style chalets. Friendly staff create a charming, homey atmosphere that enhances relaxation. The choice of daily healthy activities includes mountain hiking, indoor swimming, indoor and outdoor tennis, racquet-ball, Nautilus, and workouts that range from high-impact aerobics to spot-toning and yoga. Hot tubs, saunas, whirlpools, steam, and massage are available to soothe body, mind, and soul. Evening lectures provide the necessary grounding to solidly integrate healthy new habits into already changing lifestyles.

Nutrition is a Lesage specialty. Delightful low-fat/high-fiber meals in ample portions help trim inches painlessly. Crowning marvelous dinners are calorie-conscious desserts. The simple but ever-popular Apple Crisp and a Tangy Banana Cheesecake belie notions that equate luscious with fattening.

Apple Crisp

Apple crisp at its best.
The crunchy topping makes this a crowd pleaser.

Preheat oven to 325°F
9″ baking pan sprayed with
    nonstick vegetable spray
Serves 6–8

4 medium apples, peeled,
cored and sliced thin
⅔ cup apple juice
¼ cup raisins
2 tbsp. honey
1 tbsp. lemon juice
2 tsp. brown sugar
2 tsp. cinnamon
½ tsp. nutmeg
⅛ tsp. cloves
⅛ tsp. allspice
⅛ tsp. ginger

Mix in a bowl until well combined.

2 tbsp. wheat germ
(optional)

Coat bottom and sides of pan with wheat germ. Pour apple mixture into pan. Prepare topping.

Topping

1 cup rolled oats
1 tbsp. whole wheat flour
½ tsp. cinnamon
¼ cup brown sugar
2 tbsp. soft butter

Combine until well blended. Spread over apple mixture. Bake for approx. 50–60 minutes, or until topping is brown.

Calories: 181

Protein: 2 g

Fat: 4 g

Cholesterol: 7 mg

Carbohydrates: 36 g

Sodium: 36 mg

Frozen Banana Mousse

*So simple and delicious no one will believe
this mousse contains only one ingredient.*

Individual dishes
Serves 6

4 sliced bananas

Freeze in a plastic bag. Remove
from freezer, thaw for 10 minutes,
then purée in blender or food
processor until smooth. Serve in
dishes and, if desired, top with
fruit, yogurt, and/or nuts.

Calories:	92
Protein:	1 g
Fat:	0.5 g
Cholesterol:	0 mg
Carbohydrates:	23 g
Sodium:	1 mg

Blueberry Honey Cake

Delicious for breakfast or dessert.

Preheat oven to 350°F
9″ baking pan
Serves 6–8

1 cup fresh or frozen blueberries *⅓ cup honey* *⅓ cup water*	Place in saucepan and bring to a gentle boil.
1 tbsp. cornstarch or arrowroot	Mix with a little cold water to make a paste, then add to above mixture. Stir constantly, until thickened, then remove from heat. Set aside.
1½ cups whole wheat flour *1 tsp. baking powder*	Mix in large bowl.
1 cup milk *⅓ cup honey* *1 tbsp. oil*	Combine in another bowl, then add to flour mixture, stirring to blend. Pour into pan. Pour berry mixture over top. Bake for approx. 25–35 minutes, or until tester comes out clean.

Calories:	176
Protein:	5 g
Fat:	3 g
Cholesterol:	2 mg
Carbohydrates:	36 g
Sodium:	24 mg

Tangy Banana Cheesecake

*A creamy, tangy cheesecake that can be
beautifully decorated with berries of your choice.*

Preheat oven to 375°F
9″ pie pan sprayed with
   nonstick vegetable spray and
   coated with wheat germ if desired
Serves 6–8

1 cup cottage cheese **1 cup yogurt** **2 egg whites** **juice of ½ lemon** **1 tsp. vanilla**	Process until smooth in blender or food processor.
¼ cup & 1 tbsp. whole wheat flour	Add and continue to blend.
4 tbsp. honey	Add slowly and blend well.
2 ripe bananas	Add and continue to process until smooth. Pour into pan. Bake approx. 30–40 minutes, or until pie is firm. Chill at least 1 hour before serving.
Banana slices or berries to garnish	

Calories: 100

Protein: 6 g

Fat: 1 g

Cholesterol: 3 mg

Carbohydrates: 18 g

Sodium: 120 mg

A   Almond Vanilla Snaps   57
Angel Food Cake with Pears Puréed   133
Angel Food Chocolate Cake   42
Angel Food Strawberry Shortcake   40
Apple
  Apple Blueberry Crisp   118
  Apple Blueberry Sorbet   37
  Apple Cakes, Sweet Individual   54
  Apple Crisp   146
  Apple Crunchy Cobbler   81
  Apple Pear Croustade   36
  Apple Strudel with Cinnamon Sauce   130
  Apples, Connecticut Baked with Spa Cream   108
  Apples, Hot Spiced over Honey Vanilla Ice Cream   16
  Applesauce Carrot Cake   129
  Applesauce Spice Cake   67
Apricot Fluffy Soufflé with Raspberry Sauce   80

B   Baked Alaska   41
Baked Apples Connecticut with Spa Cream   108
Baked Banana with Cinnamon and Apple Cider   87
Baked Cinnamon Fruit Coupe   48
Baklava   93
Banana
  Banana Baked with Cinnamon and Apple Cider   87
  Banana Cake with Lemon Cream Frosting   132
  Banana Crêpes with Orange Sauce   138
  Banana Frozen Mousse   147
  Banana-Strawberry Mousse   100
  Banana Tangy Cheesecake   149
  Banana Walnut Bread   68
  Bananas Flambé   70
Berry Strudel with Papaya Sauce   61
Blintzes, Fruit   30

Blueberry
 Blueberry Apple Crisp   118
 Blueberry Apple Sorbet   37
 Blueberry Cheesecake   20
 Blueberry Crêpes   47
 Blueberry Honey Cake   148
 Blueberry, Hot Cobbler   92
 Blueberry Nut Cake   123
 Blueberry Yogurt Sauce with Poached Pears   17
Bread, Banana Walnut   68
Bread, Zucchini Pineapple   26
Brownies, Chocolate   136
Buttermilk Carrot Cake   23
Buttermilk Strawberry Orange Sorbet   84
Butternut Squash Flan   115

C   Cakes
 Angel Food Cake with Puréed Pears   133
 Angel Food Strawberry Shortcake   40
 Applesauce Carrot Cake   129
 Applesauce Spice Cake   67
 Banana Cake with Lemon Cream Frosting   132
 Blueberry Honey Cake   148
 Blueberry Nut Cake   123
 Carrot Buttermilk Cake   23
 Chiffon Cake   98
 Chocolate Angel Food Cake   42
 "Chokolate" Carob Cake with Pastry Cream   21
 Cinnamon Date Coffee Cake   137
 Cinnamon Fig Cake   76
 Coffee Chiffon Cake   15
 Individual Sweet Apple Cakes   54
 Orange Coffee Cake   119
Cal-a-Vie   111
Canyon Ranch   19

Carob "Chokolate" Cake with Pastry Cream   21
Carrot
    Carrot Applesauce Cake   129
    Carrot Buttermilk Cake   23
Cheesecake
    Cheesecake, Blueberry   20
    Cheesecake, La Costa with Strawberry Sauce   78
    Cheesecake, Light and Lovely   63
    Cheesecake, No Bake Pineapple   101
    Cheesecake, Pumpkin   24
    Cheesecake, Raspberry   34
    Cheesecake, Tangy Banana   149
    Cheesecakes, Individual Miniature   66
Chewy Cottage Cheese Cookies   74
Chiffon Cake   98
Chiffon Coffee Cake   15
Chiffon, Frozen Lemon with Berry Sauce   58
Chilled Mocha Mousse   59
Chocolate
    Chocolate Angel Food Cake   42
    Chocolate Brownies   136
    Chocolate Mousse, Five Minute   43
    Chocolate, Pots of   99
    Chocolate Sauce, Poached Pears in   51
    Chocolate Seashells   35
    Chocolate Swirl Pie   113
    "Chokolate" Carob Cake with Pastry Cream   21
Cinnamon
    Cinnamon and Apple Cider with Baked Banana   87
    Cinnamon Baked Fruit Coupe   48
    Cinnamon Fig Cake   76
    Cinnamon Honey Custard with Maple Syrup Sauce   109
    Cinnamon Sauce with Apple Strudel   130
Cobbler, Crunchy Apple   81
Cobbler, Hot Blueberry   92

Cocoa Kisses   56
Coffee Chiffon Cake   15
Coffee Cake, Cinnamon Date   137
Coffee Orange Cake   119
Cold fruit desserts
    Fruit Coulis (Purée)   144
    Fruit Kabobs with Raspberry Sauce   83
    Fruit Mosaic with Sabayon Sauce   116
    Fruit Soup   96
    Fruit Terrine with Raspberry Sauce   86
    Honey Glazed Pineapple with Strawberries   18
    Key Lime Dessert   25
    Lemon Frost   22
    Melon Balls with Warm Ginger Sauce   89
    Pineapple Lime Sorbet   110
    Poached Pear with Raspberry Purée   106
    Poached Pears in Chocolate Sauce   51
    Poached Pears with Blueberry Yogurt Sauce   17
    Raisin Rice Pudding   28
    Strawberries Grand Marnier   143
    Strawberries Romanoff   29
Connecticut Baked Apples with Spa Cream   108
Cookies and bars
    Chewy Cottage Cheese Cookies   74
    Chocolate Seashells   35
    Cocoa Kisses   56
    Crisp Nut Cookies   60
    Date Nut Bar   125
    Lady Fingers   62
    Oatmeal Maple Raisin Cookies   53
    Oatmeal Raisin Cookies   107
    Peanut Butter Cookies   72
    Peanut Butter Granola Rolls   131
    Raisin Honey Cookies   73
    Tulip Cookies with Fruit Sorbet   120

Vanilla Almond Snaps   57
Coulis Fruit Purée   144
Crêpes   31
Crêpes, Banana with Orange Sauce   138
Crêpes, Blueberry   47
Crêpes, Strawberry or Peach   127
Crêpes Suzette   46
Crisp, Apple   146
Crisp, Blueberry Apple   118
Crisp Nut Cookies   60
Croustade, Pear Apple   36
Crunchy Apple Cobbler   81
Custard, Honey Cinnamon with Maple Syrup Sauce   109

D   Date Nut Bar   125
Doral Saturnia   117

F   Fig Cinnamon Cake   76
Five Minute Chocolate Mousse   43
Flan, Butternut Squash   115
Flan, Maple with Walnuts   122
Flan, Pumpkin   128
Flans—see also "Pies, tarts, and flans"
Floating Islands with Raspberry Fruit Soup   88
Fluffy Apricot Soufflé with Raspberry Sauce   80
Four Seasons Resort and Club   13
Fresh Fruit Sorbet   27
Fresh Fruit Tart   69
Frost, Lemon   22
Frosting, Lemon Cream with Banana Cake   132
Frozen Banana Mousse   147
Frozen Jamoca Mousse   124
Frozen Lemon Chiffon with Berry Sauce   58
Frozen Lemon Roulade   140
Frozen Orange Cream   126

Frozen Vanilla Yogurt with Fresh Fruit   95
Fruit—see also "Cold fruit desserts," "Hot fruit desserts"
Fruit Blintzes   30
Fruit Coulis Purée   144
Fruit Coupe Baked Cinnamon   48
Fruit Fresh Tart   69
Fruit Kabobs with Raspberry Sauce   83
Fruit Mosaic with Sabayon Sauce   116
Fruit Mousse, Mixed   44
Fruit Sorbet, Fresh   27
Fruit Sorbet with Tulip Cookies   120
Fruit Soup   96
Fruit Soup, Raspberry, with Floating Islands   88
Fruit Terrine with Raspberry Sauce   86
Fruit, Fresh with Frozen Vanilla Yogurt   95

G   Ginger Sauce, Warm, with Melon Balls   89
Golden Door   33
Grand Marnier Orange Sorbet   38
Grand Marnier Strawberries   143
Granola, Homemade Crunchy   82
Granola Peanut Butter Rolls   131
Greenhouse, The   79
Gurney's Inn   97

H   Heartland, The   121
Homemade Crunchy Granola   82
Honey Blueberry Cake   148
Honey Cinnamon Custard with Maple Syrup Sauce   109
Honey Glazed Pineapple with Strawberries   18
Honey Raisin Cookies   73
Honey Vanilla Ice Cream with Hot Spiced Apples   16
Hot fruit desserts
    Apple Crisp   146
    Apple Strudel with Cinnamon Sauce   130

Baked Banana with Cinnamon and Apple Cider   87
Baked Cinnamon Fruit Coupe   48
Banana Crêpes with Orange Sauce   138
Bananas Flambé   70
Berry Strudel with Papaya Sauce   61
Blueberry Apple Crisp   118
Connecticut Baked Apples with Spa Cream   108
Crunchy Apple Cobbler   81
Fluffy Apricot Soufflé with Raspberry Sauce   80
Fruit Blintzes   30
Hot Blueberry Cobbler   92
Hot Spiced Apples over Honey Vanilla Ice Cream   16
Pear Apple Croustade   36

I   Ice Cream, Honey Vanilla with Hot Spiced Apples   16
Ices, sorbets, sherbets, ice milk, parfaits
Blueberry Apple Sorbet   37
Fresh Fruit Sorbet   27
Frozen Jamoca Mousse   124
Frozen Lemon Chiffon with Berry Sauce   58
Frozen Lemon Roulade   140
Frozen Orange Cream   126
Frozen Vanilla Yogurt with Fresh Fruit   95
Mocha Parfait   112
Orange Grand Marnier Sorbet   38
Orange Kiwi Sorbet   114
Pineapple Lime Sorbet   110
Raspberry Cream Sorbet   64
Raspberry Ice with Fresh Strawberries   94
Strawberry Orange Buttermilk Sorbet   84
Strawberry Orange Sorbet   37
Strawberry Rhubarb Parfait   105
Individual Miniature Cheesecakes   66
Individual Sweet Apple Cakes   54

J   Jamoca Frozen Mousse   124
Jimmy Lesage's New Life Spa   145

K   Key Lime Dessert   25
King Ranch Health Spa and Fitness Resort   135
Kiwi, Orange Sorbet   114

L   La Costa Hotel and Spa   75
La Costa Cheesecake with Strawberry Sauce   78
Lady Fingers   62
Lemon Cream Frosting with Banana Cake   132
Lemon Frost   22
Lemon, Frozen Chiffon with Berry Sauce   58
Lemon, Frozen Roulade   140
Lemon Meringue Pie   14
Light and Lovely Cheesecake   63
Lime, Key, Dessert   25
Lime Pineapple Sorbet   110

M   Maine Chance Fitness and Beauty Resort   91
Maple Flan with Walnuts   122
Maple Oatmeal Raisin Cookies   53
Maple Syrup Sauce with Honey Cinnamon Custard   109
Melba Meringues   104
Melon Balls with Warm Ginger Sauce   89
Mixed Fruit Mousse   44
Mocha Mousse Chilled   59
Mocha Parfait   112
Mousse, Banana Strawberry   100
Mousse, Chocolate Five Minute   43
Mousse, Frozen Banana   147
Mousse, Frozen Jamoca   124
Mousse, Mixed Fruit   44
Mousse, Mocha Chilled   59

N New Life Spa   145
       No Bake Pineapple Cheesecake   101
       Norwich Inn and Spa   103
       Nut Date Bar   125

O Oatmeal Maple Raisin Cookies   53
       Oatmeal Raisin Cookies   107
       Orange Coffee Cake   119
       Orange, Frozen Cream   126
       Orange Grand Marnier Sorbet   38
       Orange Kiwi Sorbet   114
       Orange Sauce with Banana Crêpes   138
       Orange Strawberry Buttermilk Sorbet   84
       Orange Strawberry Sorbet   37
       Orange Yogurt Cream   142

P Palm-Aire Resort and Spa   39
       Papaya Sauce with Berry Strudel   61
       Parfait, Mocha   112
       Parfait, Strawberry Rhubarb   105
       Parfaits—see also "Ices, sorbets, sherbets, ice milk, parfaits"
       Pastry Cream with "Chokolate" Carob Cake   21
       Peach Melba   77
       Peach or Strawberry Crêpes   127
       Peanut Butter Cookies   72
       Peanut Butter Granola Rolls   131
       Pear Apple Croustade   36
       Pears
           Poached, with Blueberry Yogurt Sauce   17
           Poached, in Chocolate Sauce   51
           Poached, with Raspberry Purée   106
           Puréed, with Angel Food Cake   133
       Pies, tarts, and flans
           Butternut Squash Flan   115
           Chocolate Swirl Pie   113

      Fresh Fruit Tart   69
      Lemon Meringue Pie   14
      Maple Flan with Walnuts   122
      Pumpkin Flan   128
      Strawberry Cheese Tart   52
      Tarte Tartin   36
Pineapple
      Pineapple, Honey Glazed with Strawberries   18
      Pineapple Lime Sorbet   110
      Pineapple, No Bake Cheesecake   101
      Pineapple Zucchini Bread   26
Poached Pears in Chocolate Sauce   51
Poached Pears with Blueberry Yogurt Sauce   17
Poached Pear with Raspberry Purée   106
Pointe, The   49
Pots of Chocolate   99
Pudding, Raisin Rice   28
Pumpkin Cheesecake   24
Pumpkin Flan   128
Purée, Raspberry with Poached Pear   106

R   Raisin Honey Cookies   73
      Raisin Oatmeal Cookies   107
      Raisin Oatmeal Maple Cookies   53
      Raisin Rice Pudding   28
      Rancho La Puerta   139
      Raspberry Cheesecake   34
      Raspberry Cream Sorbet   64
      Raspberry Fruit Soup with Floating Islands   88
      Raspberry Ice with Fresh Strawberries   94
      Raspberry Purée with Poached Pear   106
      Raspberry Sauce with Fluffy Apricot Soufflé   80
      Raspberry Sauce with Fruit Kabobs   83
      Raspberry Sauce with Fruit Terrine   86
      Rhubarb Strawberry Parfait   105

Rice Raisin Pudding   28
Romanoff, Strawberries   29
Roulade, Frozen Lemon   140

S   Sabayon Sauce with Fruit Mosaic   116
Safety Harbor Spa and Fitness Center   65
Sauces
    Berry Sauce with Frozen Lemon Chiffon   58
    Blueberry Yogurt Sauce with Poached Pears   17
    Chocolate Sauce, Poached Pears in   51
    Cinnamon Sauce with Apple Strudel   130
    Maple Syrup Sauce with Honey Cinnamon Custard   109
    Orange Sauce with Banana Crêpes   138
    Papaya Sauce with Berry Strudel   61
    Raspberry Sauce with Fluffy Apricot Soufflé   80
    Raspberry Sauce with Fruit Kabobs   83
    Raspberry Sauce with Fruit Terrine   86
    Sabayon Sauce with Fruit Mosaic   116
    Strawberry Sauce with La Costa Cheesecake   78
    Warm Ginger Sauce with Melon Balls   89
Sheraton Bonaventure Resort and Spa   45
Sherbets—see "Ices, sorbets, sherbets, ice milk, parfaits"
Shortcake, Strawberry   141
Shortcake, Strawberry Angel Food   40
Snaps, Vanilla Almond   57
Sonoma Mission Inn   55
Sorbet, Blueberry Apple   37
Sorbet, Fresh Fruit   27
Sorbet, Fruit with Tulip Cookies   120
Sorbet, Orange Grand Marnier   38
Sorbet, Orange Kiwi   114
Sorbet, Pineapple Lime   110
Sorbet, Raspberry Cream   64
Sorbet, Strawberry Orange   84
Sorbet, Strawberry Orange Buttermilk   84

Sorbets—see also "Ices, sorbets, sherbets, ice milk, parfaits"
Soufflé, Fluffy Apricot with Raspberry Sauce   80
Soup, Fruit   96
Soup, Raspberry Fruit with Floating Islands   88
Spice Cake, Applesauce   67
Squash, Butternut Flan   115
Strawberries
    Strawberries, Fresh, with Raspberry Ice   94
    Strawberries Grand Marnier   143
    Strawberries Romanoff   29
    Strawberries with Honey Glazed Pineapple   18
    Strawberry Angel Food Shortcake   40
    Strawberry Banana Mousse   100
    Strawberry Cheese Tart   52
    Strawberry or Peach Crêpes   127
    Strawberry Orange Buttermilk Sorbet   84
    Strawberry Orange Sorbet   37
    Strawberry-Rhubarb Parfait   105
    Strawberry Sauce with La Costa Cheesecake   78
    Strawberry Shortcake   141
Strudel, Apple with Cinnamon Sauce   130
Strudel, Berry with Papaya Sauce   61

T   Tangy Banana Cheesecake   149
Tart, Fresh Fruit   69
Tart, Strawberry Cheese   52
Tarte Tartin   36
Tarts—see also "Pies, tarts, and flans"
Topnotch at Stowe Resort and Spa   85
Tulip Cookies with Fruit Sorbet   120
Turnberry Isle Yacht and Country Club   71

V   Vanilla Almond Snaps   57
Vanilla Frozen Yogurt with Fresh Fruit   95

W   Walnut Banana Bread   68
         Walnuts with Maple Flan   122

Y   Yogurt, Frozen Vanilla with Fresh Fruit   95
         Yogurt, Orange Cream   142
         Yogurt, Sauce, Blueberry with Poached Pears   17

Z   Zucchini Pineapple Bread   26